THE ROTTWEILER

Tracy Libby

The Rottweiler

Project Team
Editor: Heather Russell-Revesz
Copy Editor: Joann Woy
Indexer: Lucie Haskins
Design: Tilly Grassa, TGCreative Services
Series Design: Mada Design
Series Originator: Dominique De Vito

TFH Publications®
President/CEO: Glen S. Axelrod
Executive Vice President: Mark E. Johnson
Editor-in-Chief: Albert Connelly, Jr.
Production Manager: Kathy Bontz

TFH Publications, Inc.®
One TFH Plaza
Third and Union Avenues
Neptune City, NJ 07753

ISBN 978-0-7938-3649-9

Printed and bound in China
13 14 15   9 11 12 10 8

Library of Congress Cataloging-in-Publication Data

Libby, Tracy, 1958-
  The rottweiler / Tracy Libby.
      p. cm.
  Includes index.
  ISBN 0-7938-3649-2 (alk. paper)
  1. Rottweiler dog. I. Title.
  SF429.R7L53 2005
  636.73—dc22
  2005024348

The Leader In Responsible Animal Care For Over 50 Years!®
www.tfh.com

TABLE OF CONTENTS

1

HISTORY
of the Rottweiler

W hen you look at the Rottweiler who shares your life today—lounging on the couch, riding in the car, swimming in the family pool—it may be difficult to visualize his life 2,000 years ago as a full-time working dog who was proficient at moving cattle over rough and mountainous terrain and protecting his master from predators. Of course, back then the Rottweiler breed we know and love today did not yet exist. The Rottweiler's ancestors were working dogs—but they were not always Rottweilers!

Over the years, various theories and a great deal of speculation have been put forth regarding the Rottweiler's ancestors and his precise origin; these speculations have, naturally, sparked heated and spirited debates. It is safe to say that the history of the Rottweiler is not a documented record. Much of what we know about the breed, as with most old breeds, is shrouded in mystery, with little or no documented facts for verification. What owners and historians must rely on has been passed down through history—mostly through nineteenth century legends and by word of mouth—from those who had the opportunity to know the breed long before our time.

ORIGINS OF THE ROTTWEILER

No real historic viable claim can be made that the dogs used during the Roman Empire, such as those dogs used during Caesar's two campaigns to Britain in 55 and 54 BC or the conquest of Gaul in 50 BC, were early manifestations of the Rottweiler breed. That said, what breed historians assume to be true is that the Rottweiler probably descended from a drover dog indigenous to ancient Rome. One ancestor of the Rottweiler is believed to be the intelligent Mastiff type-dog who was willing to work and possessed a strong guarding instinct. During the Roman campaigns in Europe, these drover dogs accompanied large armies of Roman soldiers during their invasions of European countries. These types of dogs were needed for their proficiency at herding cattle, as well as protecting the camp from marauders. It is not difficult to imagine that these dogs probably performed a major role in the success of these forays because of their intelligence, stamina, and great strength.

How the Rottweiler Got His Name

Around the period of AD 700, the old Roman name for the town of Arae Flaviae was replaced by the German name das Rote Wil—after the red tiles and bricks used in the buildings. The name, it is said, eventually evolved into Rottweil. Here, an outstanding dog began to develop into the Rottweiler we know and love today, although it would be many, many years before the Rottweiler actually began to resemble the breed we recognize today as the modern-day Rottweiler.

Rottweil, Germany

The Alps had been under Roman control for about 75 years when the Roman army traveled through Wurttemberg and on to the small town of Rottweil in southwestern Germany, at around AD 74. This is a period of interest to historians and Rottweiler enthusiasts. At that time, the new territory, which had natural advantages of climate, soil, and a central location, was known as Arae Flaviae. Conquered by the Romans, this area held a small fort on a military road. This fort was designated an Imperial Roman City, and it eventually became a trading and administrative center where military units were often stationed.

For the next two centuries, it is believed that the Roman drover dogs continued to guard herds of cattle in Arae Flaviae. Around AD 260, the Roman army, under pressure from Suebi and Alemanni tribes, was ousted and eventually withdrew from the area. However, agriculture and the trading of cattle remained prime occupations, and historians believe that many of these Roman drover dogs and their offspring remained in the area when the Roman soldiers moved on. It is reasonable to assume that they would have continued their work as guard and cattle dogs, controlling cattle in the butcher's yard, driving cattle from town to town, and pulling the butcher's meat-laden carts.

Switzerland's Influence

Other parts of Europe produced similar dogs who were equally capable of herding cattle and guarding their masters. They looked a bit different, with variations of size, coat type and color, but the basic function of these fearless dogs remained the same.

Rottweil began to emerge as a market town, and cattle dealers from as far away as France, Switzerland, and Hungary are believed to have bought and sold in the Rottweil market. Butchers, farmers, and cattle dealers began converging on the area in increasing numbers and, as a result, historians believe that the need grew for dogs who could drive and control cattle, as well as protect both cattle and drovers from predators and marauders.

It is worth noting that farmers and butchers were not concerned with pedigrees. Any dog who offered any chance of improving the needed characteristics would be used extensively. It is therefore possible that new bloodlines were introduced when the Rottweilers' ancestors interbred with those Swiss dogs who brought cattle down from the Swiss mountains.

History in the Making

Much of what we know about dogs during Roman times is based on literary evidence rather than archeological evidence. History, however, is never static; the passage of time, coupled with science and technology, hopefully will lead to further discoveries that will allow us to look back in time and write the final chapter on the origins of the remarkable animal we know and love as the Rottweiler. Unfortunately, just as we may never know for certain whether George Washington really cut down that infamous cherry tree, we may never know for certain the true origin of the Rottweiler breed.

The modern-day Rottweiler is a product of Germany and German breeders.

MODERN-DAY ROTTWEILERS

What historians do know for certain is that the modern-day Rottweiler is a product of Germany and those German breeders who came along many, many years after the fall of the Roman Empire.

The Rottweiler was used as a herding and drover dog until the mid-1800s but, despite his valuable attributes, developing railroads resulted in a different form of cattle transportation. Donkeys or ponies took over the task of pulling carts, and the Rottweiler, deprived of two of his principal forms of usefulness, was suddenly unemployed. Legend claims that only one Rottweiler was left in Rottweil by 1905. Unlike today, when most dogs are kept as companions, the economics of bygone eras demanded dogs earn their keep or there was no reason to keep them.

A renewed interest in the breed emerged in the

early 1900s, and by 1910 the Rottweiler—with his protective and stable nature and exemplary character—was officially recognized by the German Police Dog Association. The breed excelled at police work and, in a relatively short time, the Rottweiler emerged from obscurity.

During that time, the dog fancier also arrived on the scene, and these enthusiasts set about preserving, refining, and improving the Rottweiler breed in the form in which it was handed down to them. Several Rottweiler clubs also began to emerge, including the International Club for Leonberger and Rottweiler dogs in 1899, but it was short lived. The Deutsche Rottweiler Club was formed in 1907, followed by the South German Rottweiler Club, and then a third breed club—the International Rottweiler Club, which eventually absorbed the South German Rottweiler Club. Each of these clubs

Kennel clubs are organizations devoted to the advancement of purebred dogs.

kept stud books, and dissension was not uncommon, with clubs often disagreeing when it came to the vision of the perfect Rottweiler.

The Deutsche Rottweiler Club and the International Rottweiler Club eventually merged to form the Allgemeiner Deutscher Rottweiler Klub (ADRK), whose motto became "The Breeding of Rottweilers is the Breeding of Working Dogs." Since its 1921 inception—and despite difficulties encountered during and in the aftermath of World War II—the ADRK has remained intact and is still the governing Rottweiler club of Germany today.

ROTTWEILERS IN AMERICA

Many fine dogs, along with their breed standards, found their way to the United States from England and Europe in the mid- to late 1800s and early 1900s. The first known Rottweilers in the United States were brought over by three German immigrants in 1928. These Germans were members of the ADRK, and the first known litter of Rottweilers whelped in the US was produced by one of their bitches, in 1930. At that time, the American Kennel Club (AKC) did not yet recognize the breed, and the litter was recorded by the German Stud Book of the ADRK. Not until 1931 was the first Rottweiler— owned by August Knecht (one of the German immigrants)— registered by the AKC and admitted to the stud book, even though there was no AKC standard for the Rottweiler. That same year, 1931, the AKC registered its first litter of Rottweilers. The first AKC Rottweiler standard was adopted in 1935.

The breed remained virtually unknown in the United States until after World War II. In the 1950s, the breed began to gain in popularity, and three clubs—the Colonial Rottweiler Club on the East Coast, the Medallion Rottweiler Club in the Chicago area, and the Golden State Rottweiler Club in California—made strong efforts to improve the breed, educate the public, and develop a mandatory code of ethics. The American Rottweiler Club (ARC) was established in 1973, and it remains the breed's AKC national parent club.

The "golden age"—the years between 1960 and 1980—was considered a period of real development, optimism, and significance for the Rottweiler. A relatively small group of devoted fanciers across the country had a sincere love of the breed, a major concern for its well being, and they were all dedicated to breeding better dogs.

The Rottweiler started to gain real popularity in the mid-1980s as the perceived need for protection and guard dogs increased, and the price of Rottweilers soared. Breeds become fashionable for a variety of reasons and when they do, greed comes into play. Unscrupulous owners began breeding Rottweilers strictly for profit and, in turn, new owners who had just shelled out a bundle for a new puppy felt compelled to breed their dog to get a return on their investment. By the mid-1990s, the Rottweiler was the second most popular breed with the AKC, which registered more than 100,000 Rottweilers in 1994. In 1995, the AKC registered 93,656 Rottweilers and more than 30,950 litters. This was a tremendous explosion in popularity when one considers that 15 years earlier, in 1980, only 4,701 Rottweilers were registered with the AKC.

The Rottweiler's traditionally calm and stable temperament began to deteriorate. A surge of poorly bred Rottweilers brought infamy to the breed, as bites and maulings made the six o'clock news. The Rottweiler became the media's poster dog for hyping dangerous breeds and their bad-boy image. Breed-specific legislation aimed at the Rottweiler emerged, insurance companies started refusing homeowners' insurance, and by the late 1990s the breed's popularity began to wane. Currently, only about 17,500 dogs are registered with the AKC.

Today, knowledgeable breeders dedicated to the well being of the breed—those who have seen the breed through the best and worst of times—continue to work diligently to educate the public, maintain the breed's heritage and working ability, and preserve the valuable Rottweiler for future generations.

Believe It or Not...

Many tales abound in the history of the Rottweiler, and one often-repeated story is that these butcher dogs—or Metzgerhunds, as they became known—were used to safeguard the cash from the sale of cattle. Legend has it that lone drovers tied the money from the sale of cattle in a purse or moneybag around the dog's neck, where it was safe should any thieves be encountered along the lonely trails.

CHARACTERISTICS
of the Rottweiler

Every breed has a blueprint for success. This blueprint is called the *breed standard*, and it describes the perfect dog to which breeders aspire and against which judges compare the dogs exhibited before them. To the newcomer, it may seem nothing more than a cluster of strange-sounding words strung together on a piece of paper. However, it is a detailed description of the perfect canine specimen, describing everything from height, weight, color and coat, to angulation of limbs, eye size, color, and shape, and what a dog should look like when he is coming and going. The Rottweiler, like all breeds of dog, was developed for a particular task, and each characteristic of the breed listed in the standard is there for a purpose—to enable the dog to carry out the tasks for which he was originally bred and to accomplish these tasks with the greatest amount of ease.

A breed standard serves not only as a gauge for breeders and judges—to help them determine the ideal quality, soundness, and beauty of the Rottweiler—but also functions as a historical document. It is a document that can teach canine enthusiasts about the origin of the Rottweiler, where the breed has been, and where the breed is going. In 1883, for instance, the ideal height and weight of the Rottweiler was about 23.5 inches (59.7 cm) and 66 pounds (29.9 kg), which is about half the weight of today's male Rottweilers.

THREE STANDARDS

The first detailed description of the Rottweiler was written by Albert Kull in 1883 and published in 1901 by the International Club for Leonberger and Rottweiler dogs—a club that Kull founded in 1899. The club had a short life. Not until 1921, when two other clubs—the Deutsche Rottweiler Club and the International Rottweiler Club, both having similar breed standards—merged and formed the Allgemeiner Deutscher Rottweiler Klub (ADRK) that a mutual standard combining both working and showing abilities was agreed upon. The ADRK has remained the parent club of the Rottweiler since that time, and the standard remains the official standard of the German Rottweiler. Here's where it can be a bit confusing to newcomers: The Federation Cynologique

Proper Structure

The demands put on today's Rottweilers are a far cry from the breed's full-time job hundreds of years ago. However, proper structure is as equally important today as it was in AD 74 when the fearless Roman drover dog, the progenitor of the Rottweiler, made the trek from Rome to the banks of the Neckar River. Structurally correct Rottweilers have the physical capabilities to perform their jobs with the greatest amount of ease, be it obedience, agility, herding, police work, or daily jogs with their owners.

Internationale (FCI) is the umbrella organization for about 80 kennel clubs around the world, but it is the country of origin of a breed that oversees their country's breed standards. Because Germany is the mother country, and the ADRK is the responsible club in Germany, the Rottweiler breed standard is frequently referred to as the ADRK or the German standard, but the official term is "FCI standard."

In addition to the FCI standard, a British breed standard is controlled by the UK's Kennel Club (KC), and an American breed standard is overseen by the Rottweiler's national parent club, the American Rottweiler Club (ARC) and guided by the American Kennel Club (AKC). With the exception of minor variations, the three standards describe the same dog. The primary difference between the standards is the amount of detailed description and their phraseology.

BREED TYPE

When you see a Rottweiler, you know he is a Rottweiler without consciously stopping to think about it. But how? How do you know he is a Rottweiler and not, say, a Doberman or a Labrador Retriever? Is it the dog's color? Size? Self-assured presence? One is not likely to confuse a Rottweiler with a Pembroke Welsh Corgi, even though both dogs were originally used as herding dogs. What separates one breed from another are the breeds' individual attributes and characteristics. These attributes and characteristics are called *breed type*—or in canine terminology, the essence of the breed.

Breed type is rooted in a breed's origin—the original purpose and function of a breed. The Rottweiler has identifiable characteristics, such as size, substance, and temperament, that were developed for a specific purpose and bred into the breed long enough for these characteristics to become stable, recognizable, and reproducible with some uniformity. These individual attributes and characteristics are unique to the Rottweiler breed. They are the distinguishing features that help you to recognize a Rottweiler as being a Rottweiler.

Character and Temperament

One of the most important breed characteristics of the Rottweiler is his character and temperament. Think back to the Rottweiler's original purpose and function. His origin is from the Roman times, an era in which he was used as a herder for cattle and as a drover's dog. He defended his master and his master's property—perhaps including cash from the sale of cattle. Specific characteristics were required to fulfill the breed's role as companion, guardian, and working dog. He needed to be strong, sturdy, dependable, courageous, self-assured, and intelligent. He also needed to think for himself, because he often worked out of sight of his master. The AKC breed standard describes his temperament as being a "calm, confident, and courageous dog with a self-assured aloofness that does not lend itself to immediate and indiscriminate friendships. A Rottweiler is self-confident and responds quietly and with a wait-and-see attitude to influences in his environment."

The breed standard describes the ideal quality, soundness, and beauty of the Rottweiler.

While today's Rottweilers are more closely associated with their military and guard dog heritage than their herding roots, the breed remains a versatile, athletic dog who should be capable of herding a flock of sheep or cattle, pulling a cart with a load, tracking a lost person, and, ultimately, being a devoted and loyal companion and protector.

The Rottweiler was never meant to be a fighting dog, and he should not be nervous or aggressive, but should have natural guarding instincts and an inherent desire to protect home and family. It is his good nature, outstanding character, and devoted companionship that have endeared the breed to his owners for over 100 years.

Balance and Substance

As a droving dog, the Rottweiler spent long hours behind a herd of cattle, and his movement needed to be balanced, harmonious, powerful, and unhindered so that he could move with power and ease for many miles. To move correctly, his heavy bones and musculature needed to be balanced so that he could maintain a comfortable trotting gait all day. Few will disagree that there is no better moving dog than a well-built Rottweiler.

When you hear the Rottweiler referred to as

One of the most important breed characteristics of the Rottweiler is his character and temperament.

a "trotter"—they are referring to his gait (stride), which is outlined in the breed standard as the ideal gait for efficiency. The trot is a natural, two-beat, diagonal gait in which the front foot and the opposite hind foot work in unison, with the hind foot striking the ground a split second after the front foot. The motion is effortless and efficient, and timing and coordination must be precise.

Size Matters

The size of a Rottweiler is not necessarily a factor when it comes to the soundness of gait, because soundness, foot timing, and stride are based upon symmetry, balance, and correct structure rather than on size. That said, when one thinks of a Rottweiler, size is an important part of the Rottweiler's established breed type. Again, think about why the Rottweiler was originally developed. The forefathers of the breed were dogs of sufficient size and strength to perform guarding and herding duties. Can you imagine a 20-pound (9 kg) Rottweiler herding cattle for the Roman Army, protecting them from predators, both human and animal? Guarding his master and his master's cash? When you look at a Rottweiler, be it male or female, the dog should convey the impression that he can do his job.

Today, the ideal Rottweiler is described in the AKC and ADRK standards as a "medium-large" dog. The UK standard describes the Rottweiler as being "above average size." In addition to size, the ADRK standard lists the ideal weight of males at 50 kilos (110 pounds) and bitches at 42 kilos (92 pounds). A Rottweiler who is too big or too heavy loses his maneuverability, agility, and endurance. Equally important, an overweight Rottweiler is at risk for developing a myriad of health problems, which are discussed in subsequent chapters.

Proportion

The key component when discussing the size, height, and weight of Rottweilers is proportion. A Rottweiler must be correctly proportioned. Some call it balance, harmonious balance, or even symmetry. Regardless of the terminology, the Rottweiler must be correctly proportioned. For instance, a Rottweiler who stands 27 inches (68.5 cm) at the withers should have a body length of 30 inches (76.2 cm) because the standard says "the most desirable proportion of the height to length being [the ratio of] 9 to 10." If a Rottweiler were 27 inches (68.5 cm) tall at the withers and 42 inches (106.6 cm) long in body—it would disrupt the breed's overall appearance and harmonious balance. Despite the fact that he would not be an efficient herding dog, he would look like a Dachshund on steroids—not a Rottweiler.

The Rottweiler's forequarters and powerful hindquarters must be well proportioned and compatible, as defined in the standard, for a dog to function efficiently as a whole. If a dog's front or rear assembly are out of sync, it produces a variety of gaiting problems, which can include crabbing, overreaching, pacing, and so forth.

The same elements of proportion, which are spelled out in the breed standard, apply to a Rottweiler's topline, head, neck, chest, ears, eyes, and so forth. The proper Rottweiler head, for instance, is very distinct, with strong upper and lower jaws, and it is an essential and identifying characteristic of the breed. His zygomatic arch—his cheekbones—reflects the breed's strength and biting power. If his zygomatic arch were overdeveloped, his head would look more like that of a Bull Mastiff. If he had pronounced cheekbones and a poorly defined stop—the indentation between

A Viscious Rumor

Few can deny that today's Rottweilers maintain a physical appearance that implies a distinct intimidation factor. This should not, however, be interpreted as a dog who is bred to be vicious. The media and entertainment industry have done a great disservice to the Rottweiler by portraying the breed in movies and commercials as the stereotypical vicious, man-eating dog who roams neighborhoods consuming small children and family pets. A well-bred, well-socialized Rottweiler is good natured and has a stable temperament. The Kennel Club standard describes his characteristics as "displaying boldness and courage. Self assured and fearless. Calm gaze should indicate good humour."

Cattle Herding Rotties

Years ago, two sizes of Rottweilers existed, according to the 1926 publication *The Rottweiler in Word and Picture.* The larger, heavier Rottweiler was used for draft work, because the larger the dog, the more weight he could pull. A large dog, however, was not as advantageous when it came to working cattle. He had less maneuverability and was too heavy to spend long hours working cattle. Rather than bite cattle low on the hock, a larger dog was more inclined to bite high on the shoulder, damaging the meat. The smaller and lighter Rottweilers were used for cattle herding. Their size was better suited for this type of work because their lighter weight allowed them better endurance and agility—the ability to maneuver quickly at full speed—and restricted their bite to the lower, less valuable parts of the cattle.

the eyes where the nasal bone and skull meet—his head would look more like that of a Staffordshire Bull Terrier.

Coat and Color

A Rottweiler's coat is a true working dog coat. At the risk of sounding redundant, it is important to think about the breed's original function as a herding, draft, and guard dog. To keep him warm and dry, a Rottweiler's coat is double layered—he has a water-resistant outer coat and a shorter, insulating undercoat. His coat is designed to work as a protective covering against the elements and is capable of enduring all sorts of weather.

The glossy black outer coat is straight, coarse, dense, and of medium length with no undercoat showing through. The outer coat should feel harsh to the touch, which is frequently a surprise to newcomers. From a distance, one is likely to assume that the coat is sleek like that of a Doberman, which is incorrect. Wavy coats, excessively short, or curly coats are also faulted in the breed standard. A long coat is a disqualification.

The undercoat, which may be black, grey or tan, is often soft and woolly. It is worth noting that climatic conditions influence the amount of a dog's undercoat. A Rottweiler living in southern California will have less need for a thick undercoat than a dog living in the cold winters of, say, Montana or Alaska.

A Rottweiler's black color and rich mahogany or rust colored markings help set him apart from other breeds. While some unscrupulous breeders have marketed red Rottweilers as being rare and expensive, a Rottweiler's coat is always black. The breed's distinctive color and markings help define the Rottie's breed type and help you recognize him as a Rottweiler.

The quality and location of these rust markings is an essential part of the Rottweiler characteristics, and the demarcation between black and rust must be clearly defined. The highlight points of mahogany or rust markings are located in one spot over each eye; on the cheeks; a strip around each side of the muzzle, but not on the bridge of the nose; on the throat, and a strip on each side of the prosternum, the forelegs, the inside of the rear legs, and under the tail. The location of these markings is important, and the AKC, UK and ADRK breed standards indicate the correct amount and placement of these markings.

A Tale of Tails

Perhaps nothing is more controversial in the breed standard than the docking of a Rottweiler's tail. It is not a practice indigenous to the Rottweiler breed, but it is a tradition that has come under fire for many years. In Germany, the practice of docking tails is forbidden.

Much has been written about the history of tail docking in the Rottweiler breed, as well as in other breeds that were originally employed as herding and working dogs. Some theorize that the history of tail docking dates to the early Romans—who believed that the practice prevented rabies. There is also the theory of acquired characteristics that was debated in the late 1700s. Simply put, if the mother and father dogs had no tails—the puppies would acquire the no-tail look of their parents.

The Rottweiler's forequarters and powerful hindquarters must be proportional for him to function efficiently.

Perhaps the most common accumulated traditions and beliefs are those associated with working, herding, and hunting dogs. Docking the tails of livestock dogs was a common practice among herdsmen 150 years ago, and legend has it that these dogs were exempt from a luxury tax that was imposed on owners of nonworking dogs. As a result, owners of working dogs docked their dogs' tails as a way to document the dogs' lawful and tax-free occupation. These dogs frequently worked in varying environmental conditions, and it is believed a dog's tail was docked to reduce his susceptibility to injury from dense vegetation, briars, sticks, burrs, and the like.

Another reason for docking tails, allegedly, was to reduce the number of places another dog or animal could grab. Herdsman also believed a dog's tail acted as a rudder, and they supposedly docked the tail as a way to reduce maneuverability, which was supposed to discourage a dog's fondness and inclination for chasing game.

Finally, there is the theory that tails were docked on working and herding dogs for hygienic reasons, such as preventing feces from collecting around the base of the tail, which, in addition to being generally unpleasant, could lead to bacteria accumulation, flies, and maggots.

The classic Rottweiler temperament is driven and good natured, with great courage.

The Rottweiler's tail was docked long before any parent clubs or organizations developed a breed standard, and it remains a clearly identifiable characteristic of the breed. Today's AKC breed standard clearly states that a Rottweiler's tail is docked. The UK standard permits a docked or undocked tail, but any docking must be done by a licensed veterinary surgeon. The ADRK standard was recently amended to prohibit tail docking.

Personality Profile

The breed standard describes the ideal temperament of the Rottweiler. In the real world, Rottweilers can run

Defining Temperament

Generally speaking, the best indicator of a puppy's temperament is the disposition and activity level of the mother and father. If, for example, a puppy is the product of parents who both possess exceptional temperaments, there is a high probability that the puppy will inherit the same exceptional temperament and will show his parent's influence throughout his life. Of course, exceptions to the genetic lottery exist, and some puppies, regardless of their parent's genetic contribution, grow into adult dogs with unstable temperaments. Environmental influences and the conditions under which a puppy is whelped, reared, and socialized also play an important part in defining his temperament. Most knowledgeable breeders can match the personality and temperament of a particular dog with the right family, which makes finding a knowledgeable and reputable breeder doubly important.

the gamut in temperaments, and the genetic lottery can produce Rottweilers who are good natured, mellow, shy, nervous, or fearful, as well as hyperactive or dog aggressive. Most well-bred Rottweilers acquired from reputable breeders fall somewhere in the middle and possess the classic Rottweiler temperament that is driven and good natured, with great courage.

Until the 1960s, German breeding heavily influenced the Rottweiler breed, and dogs were bred to work and perform a specific job. While their temperaments required a self-assured aloofness, which is still called for in today's breed standard, they also tended to have a suspicious nature. Generally speaking, kids did not play with the dogs. They were not bred to be teddy bears or to cuddle with their owners. Many owners believed that house pets would not work, so the breed was primarily a kennel dog, handled mainly by men.

As the breed grew in popularity in the United States, the intense working temperament called for in the breed standard was not conducive for companion pet homes. Today, most Rottweilers are kept as pets, and they live a cushier life than their forebears did 100 years ago. They sleep on couches and beds, ride in the car, go on vacation with their owners, and compete in a myriad of canine activities. An important characteristic of the breed is that he is capable of living in modern society. As a result, the stronger, harder temperaments called for in previous generations of dogs have had to change. This is a source of contention among many breeders, and it has sparked heated and spirited debates about preserving the integrity and working ability of the breed.

While they still maintain their strong, powerful, and intimidating physical appearance, today's typical Rottweilers are

gentle, playful, affectionate, and love to cuddle with their owners. Equally important, well-bred Rottweilers are still capable of performing and excelling in carting, therapy work, obedience, herding, and many other canine activities.

IS THE ROTTWEILER RIGHT FOR YOU?

With appropriate training, Rottweilers make superb companions and exceptional house dogs. Be forewarned—most Rottweilers love to be with you every minute of the day, and it is not unusual for them to be constantly underfoot. If you lie on the floor to watch television, they will lie down with you. When you are working at your computer, they will be at your feet—or more likely on your feet! When you make dinner, they will gladly lie in front of the stove or refrigerator, watching your every move—and perhaps eagerly anticipating a tidbit of food to hit the floor. They are always willing to help you fold laundry, load the dishwasher, mop the floors, and, most important, accompany you to the bathroom— regardless of how many times a day you go! If you are sick in bed, your Rottweiler will likely lie beside the bed—periodically checking on you and assessing the situation. Rottweilers are keenly in tune to their owners' mannerisms, and stories have been told about dogs sensing an impending health problem long before the owner knew anything was amiss.

It is worth noting that this is not a breed that does well unattended. They do not make good backyard dogs. Rottweilers need to be a part of the family, but they must also learn early on their place in the family hierarchy. Rottweilers are independent, dominant, and intelligent—although they can be equally stubborn, willful, and bossy, which is a result of their working background and their need to think on their own and work without assistance.

Rottweilers are also kind dogs. They are attentive to their owners, loyal, and, because of their guarding background, they are inherently protective of their home and family—always looking after them under any circumstance. Countless stories have been told of Rottweilers who have displayed great courage in protecting their owners—and anything belonging to their owner! It is not unusual to hear stories of Rottweilers who are territorial—guarding and protecting their owners while in the confines of their property—yet when outside the boundaries of their domain, they are extremely friendly and stop guarding. Put them back on their property and they are all business—willing to stand their ground and 100 percent committed to defending their property.

While most Rottweilers are not hyperactive, they do possess a moderate amount of energy. And like any energetic dog, they require both physical and mental stimulation, be it a daily walk or jog, retrieving a ball or flying disc, swimming, hiking, obedience training, herding, tracking, and so forth. Without appropriate physical and mental stimulation, Rottweilers, like most dogs, will find their own outlets for releasing pent-up energy, which frequently include destructive chewing, digging, and excessive barking.

Living Arrangements

In an ideal world, every Rottweiler would live in the country with acres of pastures and fields for running, hiking, and exploring on a daily basis with his owner. In the real world, some Rottweilers live in the country, but a large portion also live in suburbia and big cities. Some live on farms, some in condominiums. Regardless of where you live, your Rottweiler should live with you. As previously mentioned, this is not a breed that does well unattended. Rottweilers need social interaction with their owners. Despite their size, Rottweilers can and do make excellent house dogs when they receive appropriate training.

That said, you will also need a secure fenced yard or kennel area for those times when your dog must be outside to relieve himself or be left alone for short periods of time. You should never keep your Rottweiler on a chain or tie-out. This is neither fair nor humane. The fenced area must be at least 6 feet (1.8 m) tall, and equipped with secure latches or locks that intruders, curious children, or talented and determined Rottweilers cannot open. It is prudent to locate the fenced area in a portion of the yard that is not accessible to passersby. Some people, both children and adults, take great pleasure in taunting a chained or fenced dog. This can cause an otherwise well-tempered Rottweiler to become frustrated and aggressive in reaction to the abuse. It can also create myriad behavioral problems, including excessive barking.

Like humans, dogs need plenty of exercise to maintain their good health.

Regardless of whether you live in the city, suburbia, or the country, you should never allow your Rottweiler to roam at will. Unsupervised dogs may be stolen, hit by a car, poisoned, shot by neighboring farmers and ranchers, or, at the very least, develop bad habits. If you live in an apartment, condominium, or a house without a fenced yard, you will need to schedule regular outings—first thing in the morning, in the afternoon, and again in the evening. If your outings include a trip to a public dog park, be sure to follow designated rules and regulations.

The danger of allowing your Rottweiler to be exposed to excessive temperatures cannot be stressed enough. If your Rottweiler must remain outdoors for any length of time, you must provide him with plenty of fresh water, shade, and a cool spot for sleeping. You also should restrict any type of extended exercise to the cooler parts of the day.

Exercise Needs

Like humans, dogs need plenty of exercise to maintain their good health. Exercise is vital for stimulating your Rottweiler's respiratory and circulatory systems and for building strong bones and muscles. Exercise will ward off obesity—keeping your Rottweiler fit and lean. Exercise nourishes and energizes a Rottweiler's mind, keeping him active, healthy, and alert. Exercise and interactive play between a Rottweiler and his owner can help eliminate loneliness, stress, and boredom, which are often the primary causes of unwanted behaviors including destructive chewing and barking. Exercise is a great way to give your Rottie plenty of attention while building a strong human–canine relationship. Contrary to public opinion, most dogs will not run out in the backyard and exercise themselves—regardless of how big their fenced yard might be. Most generally, dogs will sit at the door—or chew and dig to entertain themselves—while they wait for their owners to come outside and play.

Any exercise program must be tailored to suit your Rottweiler—taking into account his age, health, and overall physical condition. A puppy, for instance, will tire more quickly than an adult Rottweiler. Therefore, a puppy will require short but multiple exercise periods spaced throughout the day. You also must take plenty of care with your Rottweiler puppy. He may act tough, but his body is young and tender, and he can easily be injured when jumping, twisting, turning, or getting body slammed by a bigger dog. A healthy adult Rottweiler may require more than a brisk walk around the block to satisfy his energy requirements. Again, much will depend on your dog's overall physical and mental health and individual energy level.

Equally important, do not neglect your older Rottweiler. A senior dog needs exercise to keep his body and systems functioning properly. The exercise, of course, will not be as strenuous as a younger dog's, but it should be regular exercise and enough to keep him active, alert, and healthy.

As with any exercise program, it is important to start slow and gradually work your way up to higher levels. Remember, Rottweilers do not tolerate hot temperatures and, like most breeds, are susceptible to heat stroke. So, it is best to confine your exercise and training to the cooler parts of the day. If you notice signs of fatigue, including heavy panting, you should allow your Rottweiler plenty of time to rest and cool down. If your Rottweiler is overweight, injured, or out of condition, it is prudent to consult with your veterinarian before beginning any exercise program.

Other Pets

Rottweilers, especially males, can be aggressive toward other dogs. This is why socialization is extremely important in the rearing of Rottweilers. This point cannot be overstated! Owners

No Jumping!

Rottweilers weigh quite a bit more than small children—and even some adults! For no other reason, you should train your dog early on that jumping on people is never allowed. If you own a Rottweiler, it is highly unlikely your children will survive adolescence without being knocked down a time or two. A 110-pound (49.9 kg) Rottweiler can easily—albeit accidentally—knock over a child with a simple bump.

must understand the breed's temperament and the consequences of not taking immediate action at the first sign of dominance and/or aggression toward other dogs or animals.

It is much easier to prevent aggression in puppies than to manage it in adult dogs. In adult dogs, aggression, or any undesirable behavior, is never really "cured" but merely managed.

With proper socialization and a good dose of common sense on the owners' part, most Rottweilers can and do live happily with other animals, be they other dogs, cats, goats, sheep, or pigs. Many Rottweilers accompany their owners on trail rides and happily accept horses. Many Rottweilers live on farms and in rural environments with other animals, reflecting their original purpose as herding dogs.

It is important that Rottweilers be introduced to other animals in a safe, positive, and controlled environment—a controlled environment in which the owner, and not the dog, is controlling the situation! It is about management and expectations. What type of behaviors will you accept? How about chasing, harassing, or bullying the cat, the goats, or other dogs? Hopefully not! You manage and control the situation so that your puppy is not put in the position of being allowed to develop bad or fearful behaviors.

For example, some inexperienced (or indulgent) owners find it cute when their young puppy "squares up" to an adult dog. It is far from amusing when their young dog grows into a strong, determined adult dog who challenges other dogs, is dog-to-dog aggressive, can't be taken out in public, and is eventually surrendered to the humane society or euthanized when he kills or maims another dog. On the other hand, if other dogs bully your Rottweiler puppy, he may grow into an adult dog who is afraid of other dogs.

How can you tell the difference between aggression, fear, and play? Many novice or inexperienced owners do not know what dog play looks like. Dogs run, chase, play bite, tug at body parts, yip, yap, body slam, and knock each other down. Most of the time, it's great fun for the dogs— provided both dogs are enjoying the game. So how do owners tell when a fun game has turned ugly? It's important to watch both dogs' body language—the dog chasing and the dog being chased. Are your dog's ears up? Is he returning the play? Or is one dog trying to literally run away? Is one dog nervous or frightened? Is his tail between his legs? If so, the game has crossed the line into bullying, and it's time for human intervention.

Dog-to-dog aggression also can result when owners interfere in normal dog-to-dog interactions on neutral territory. Owners will tighten up on the leash when another dog approaches. This tells the dog, "Mom is worried. Something must be wrong. I'd better protect her from this other dog."

A final note: Generally, dogs of the opposite sex are less likely to squabble or fight. Also, male-to-male aggression is different from female-to-female aggression, which is generally more intense and can end in serious injury or death.

Rottweilers and Children

If you grew up with a dog or two, no doubt you recognize the priceless education and lifelong lessons children can learn from canine companions. Rottweilers give unconditional love and companionship that can build confidence in a child. They are tireless companions and have far more energy than parents! A Rottweiler is an excellent cohort for surviving adolescence, sharing secrets, and exploring the world with guidance.

That said, buying a puppy for your children and expecting them to look after his daily needs is a fantasy that exists only in your mind. In real life, it is never practical or realistic to expect a young child to assume all the duties of rearing and caring for a dog and, more often than not, it is the dog who pays the price for the family's optimism.

Generally speaking, most good-natured Rottweilers do quite well in a household when they are raised with children, established guidelines are followed, and children are clearly supervised. Rottweilers may have been tough enough to protect cattle and Roman soldiers, but even the most accepting Rottweiler may not tolerate the rough-and-tumble behavior of young kids who try to smother him with affection, tug on his ears or tails, bang pots on his heads, or poke little fingers in his eyes. These types of behaviors can startle, frighten, and even injure a Rottweiler.

Teach Your Children Well

Parents are the key figures when it comes to teaching children how to interact safely with dogs. From day one, it is important that you teach your child some basic common courtesies that apply to the family dog just as they would to other family members. For instance, you would not allow a child to jump on a parent or sibling who is sleeping, or barge into a bathroom without knocking. The same considerations apply to the family dog, such as teaching children not to disturb a sleeping dog, or bother a dog who is eating or chewing a bone.

Teach your children always to ask permission before petting a strange dog.

Young children, generally under the age of seven, do not understand the consequences of their actions. They see nothing wrong with trying to pick up a puppy by his ears or by wrapping their arms around his neck and squeezing with all their might. They do not understand that they can seriously injure a puppy or young dog if they pick him up incorrectly or, heaven forbid, drop him.

At the other end of the spectrum, when a puppy is allowed to play unsupervised throughout his puppyhood with several young children, you end up with an adult dog who has learned to chase, jump, and nip at arms and legs, which are natural canine behaviors.

Movement stimulates a puppy's natural instinct to chase and nip and, left unchecked, your puppy will see no harm in continuing this "game" when he is a 100-pound (45.4kg) adult dog.

Equally important, infants, babies, and young children should

What Children Should Learn About Dogs

Children who are raised with dogs must understand that not all dogs are as lovable and well behaved as their own Rottweiler. Children should learn:

- To ask permission before petting a strange dog.
- To offer their hand with their palm facing up (like feeding sugar cubes to a horse). Some dogs hate to be patted on the head and will shy away or possibly nip.
- To never go into a house or yard where a dog is present unless the owners are in attendance.
- Stay away from chained, fenced, or stray dogs.
- Always get help from an adult when dealing with an injured dog, because they are more likely to bite as a reflex to the pain.
- Never stare directly at a dog. The dog may perceive this as a challenge.

never, ever, under any circumstances be left alone with a dog regardless of how trustworthy he may be. No dog is completely predictable with children. A dog may misread the strange sounds of an infant or the unpredictable behaviors of a toddler.

Children who learn to tend to the needs of their dog can learn responsibility, respect, and compassion. They learn that he needs water when he is thirsty, food when he is hungry, a bath when he is dirty, and peace and quiet when he is sleeping. At what age you begin teaching these responsibilities varies depending on the individual child. Some things you can teach a 4-year-old child, but not a 3-year-old. A child's individual maturity level dictates how much responsibility to give her in any part of life, including the responsibility of feeding and caring for a dog.

The Finer Points of Play

Play is a wonderful way to release the excess energy of both dogs and kids. They run, jump, swim, and go for bike rides. Children also need to be taught what games are and are not acceptable when playing with dogs. To prevent the situation from getting out of control, parents always should monitor and control the play between dogs and kids; play should be appropriate to the size and age of the dog as well as the child. Think active rather than rough—avoid games that encourage or allow a dog to use his teeth, such as sic 'em or attack, or wrestling games where a dog can become overexcited and inadvertently learn to use his teeth. Children should never be allowed to hit, kick, pinch, punch, bite, or harass a dog in the name of play.

PREPARING
for Your Rottweiler

O wning a dog is an enormous responsibility. Owning a big, powerful breed with big, powerful jaws and one whose physical appearance alone is capable of wrecking havoc in many a neighborhood carries an added moral and legal responsibility. There is no denying that Rottweiler puppies are irresistible with their cuddly black-bear good looks and puppyish antics. While the majority of them grow into sensitive, loving, caring companions, acquiring a Rottweiler—or any dog—on impulse is a bad idea. A well-bred and well-cared for Rottweiler can live to be 9, 10, or 11 years of age. Caring for a dog is also a lot of hard work, because he cannot take care of himself. For the next 8 to 10 years, he will depend on you for his food, water, shelter, exercise, grooming, training, affection, and regular veterinary care. He will look to you for companionship at all hours of the day. He may want to play when you want to relax. It is highly likely he will occasionally track mud through the house, refuse to come when he is called, and embarrass you in front of your friends, neighbors, and in-laws.

BEFORE YOU DECIDE

Do Your Research

You should read, observe, study, and learn everything about the breed before purchasing a Rottweiler. You must understand the Rottweiler temperament so that you can choose a dog who suits your temperament, lifestyle, and living conditions. If you and your Rottweiler have different temperaments—if, for instance, you are mellow and he is energetic, or he is very independent and strong willed and you are quiet, timid, or reserved—life will be harder for both of you. Compatible temperaments can mean the difference between a happy partnership that lasts years and a constant battle of wills that may make you wish you had gotten a cat.

If you educate yourself and make wise choices in the beginning, you greatly increase

You'll have to decide if a Rottweiler puppy or adult is right for you.

your odds of having a long, happy, and rewarding relationship with your Rottweiler.

Puppy or Adult?

Is a Rottweiler puppy or adult right for you? Here are some things to consider.

Raising a Puppy

Acquiring a Rottweiler puppy, as opposed to an older dog, allows you to start with a clean slate, so to speak. The puppy has no bad habits (yet!), and you can maximize his potential by molding his character, fostering his zany personality, and instilling all the behaviors he will need to function as he grows bigger and bolder. You can set your own expectations and manage your puppy so that he grows into a well-rounded, well-behaved adult dog.

The flip side is that raising a puppy is a lot of work. Puppies are cute and adorable for a reason; if they weren't…who in their right mind would spend 24 hours a day feeding them, cleaning up after them, and listening to them whimper and cry? Unfortunately, that is why a lot of dogs end up in humane societies and rescue groups: When the "cuteness" wears off, they are still dogs who need to be trained, groomed, fed, and loved on a daily basis.

Puppies also are demanding, and they want a lot of attention—at all hours of the day and usually in the middle of the night. Puppies don't like to be left alone. If you leave them alone, they get into all kinds of mischief—barking, chewing, digging, and peeing on the rug.

Raising a puppy is not unlike raising a human baby. You need to manage a puppy's environment 24 hours a day, so that he does not chew anything and everything in sight, pee from one end of the house to the other, or run into the street and get hit by a car. A puppy must be housetrained and obedience trained. He needs guidance and direction, so that he doesn't bark all night, chase other animals, or dig holes in your newly planted rose garden.

A Rottweiler puppy requires an enormous amount of socialization. This is essential if you plan to raise a well-behaved, nonaggressive adult Rottweiler. You will need to spend a lot of time taking him to puppy socialization classes and for walks in the park and rides in the car. You will need to expose him to every possible situation he is likely to encounter as an adult, such as kids on bicycles, joggers, women in floppy hats, other animals, trash cans, and people in wheelchairs. Raising a puppy is rewarding and a life-changing experience, but a lot of work! Don't let anyone tell you otherwise.

Adopting an Adult

Unless you have your heart set on a puppy, you might want to consider the benefits of purchasing an adult Rottweiler. When you purchase an older Rottweiler, say a 1-, 2-, or 3-year-old, what you see is what you get. An older dog's personality is already developed. With close observation, interaction, and help from a knowledgeable dog person, you should be able to determine the quality of his disposition and whether or not he will suit your personality and daily life. Is he timid? Aggressive? Bold? Does he have ants in his pants? Is he energetic? Happy? Is he spoiled rotten? Does he get along with kids? Other animals?

Adult Rottweilers become available for a variety of reasons. Many breeders, for instance, have retired show dogs they are looking to place in good companion homes. Some breeders have 1- or 2-year-old show prospects who did not pan out because of conformation faults, but who would make exceptional pets. These dogs are often obedience trained, crate trained, housetrained, and well beyond the puppy chewing stage. Occasionally, adult dogs are returned to the breeder because the owner moved or is no longer able to keep the dog. Owners often return a dog after he has outgrown the cute puppy stage, and they find themselves overwhelmed with the demands of a large, powerful dog. Many of these dogs are well bred and have been well cared for yet, for one reason or another, need to be placed in a good home.

Adult Rottweilers often are advertised "Free to Good Home" in local papers, which is code for "The dog has a lot of bad habits, he's driving me crazy, and I don't want him anymore." These dogs are often lacking in direction, management, and love, and have been allowed to develop annoying habits. In the right hands, they can make wonderful pets, but go in with your eyes wide open.

Rottweilers often are surrendered or abandoned at local humane societies. Many of these dogs are then rescued by Rottweiler rescue volunteers and placed in foster homes until permanent homes can be found.

That said, purchasing an adult dog is not without risk. A show dog who has been raised in a kennel situation will most likely be crate trained, accustomed to traveling, and oblivious to the pandemonium of shows, but he may not be housetrained. An adult dog may or may not have been raised around kids, and he may or may not like kids. Some children are more active and vocal than others, and this can intimidate or annoy even the most stable dog. If you have children, most reputable breeders will want to meet them and observe how they behave and interact around dogs, and vice versa. Absent any problems, most kids and Rottweilers who are properly introduced and supervised can develop a strong and loving relationship that will last a lifetime.

Male or Female?

When all is said and done, choosing a male or female dog usually comes down to personal preference. Some people are attracted to the large, handsome head of the males. Others love the femininity and slight refinement of the females. Both males and females can make sweet, loving companions, and the pros and cons of either sex seem to balance each other out. However, when it comes to choosing a Rottweiler, knowledgeable breeders know the capabilities of both sexes and are your best bet when it comes to assessing whether a male or female best suits your temperament, personality, and lifestyle. If you are undecided, here are a few things to consider:

- Regardless of the breed, in most instances, male dogs (and some females) will have a natural tendency to mark their territory by hiking their leg and urinating. It is a way of saying, "I was here." A Hallmark card would be nicer, but that's not the way dogs operate. They place a scent of ownership around a territory that can include sofas, laundry baskets, lawn furniture, car tires, planter boxes, and the like. Some males have been known to hike their leg on other dogs, people, and even their owner.
- Intact females (females who have not been neutered) come into heat once they have reached their sexual maturity. This usually occurs between 6 and 10 months of age, but can vary with individual females. Most females come into season about every 6 or 9 months for their entire lives. Each cycle lasts about 21 days, and during this time females become fertile and receptive to mating. The confinement of a female in heat is extremely important. Twenty-four-hour house arrest comes to mind. You must pay meticulous attention to her whereabouts at all times, because she will be irresistible to males, and vice versa. It takes only a second of miscalculated judgment on your part and you have a litter of unwanted puppies.
- Intact males are more likely than females to roam. Some intact male Rottweilers, despite their mode of containment, become talented and accomplished escape artists at the slightest whiff of a female in heat. They have been known to scale 6-foot (1.8 m) fences and chew through chain link fences. While it might seem inequitable that the female poodle in season three blocks away is wrecking havoc with your Rottweiler's good senses—ultimately the responsibility of keeping an intact male confined falls squarely on your shoulders.

Finally, when well-bred and well-socialized, the

Rottweiler breed in general is not aggressive toward other dogs. However, if you already own a dog—regardless of the breed—and are thinking of adding a Rottweiler, you should consider a dog of the opposite sex that is (or will be) spayed or neutered. If, for instance, you already own a male dog, consider getting a female. If you currently own a female, consider getting a male dog. Dogs of the opposite sex tend to wreak less havoc in terms of fighting and squabbling, and some females—despite your best intentions— simply will not live together happily. While it is possible for the experienced person to keep multiple dogs of the same sex, it is nearly impossible for the novice or inexperienced owner to restore peace on a permanent basis once problems arise. Rottweilers who fight are a danger not only to themselves but also to every member of the family. More often than not, the end result usually requires one of the dogs finding a new place to call home.

WHERE TO FIND THE ROTTWEILER OF YOUR DREAMS

The good news is you need not go to Rottweil to find the perfect Rottweiler. Finding the perfect canine companion does, however, require time, intestinal fortitude, and a bit of detective work. You must do your homework and check on resources, familiarize yourself with the Rottweiler breed standard, and research the best places to find your dog. Sadly, some people breed Rottweilers purely for money, with little interest in the future welfare of the dog. Therefore, you should talk to trainers, veterinarians, and other Rottweiler owners. You must separate opinion from fact, which can be a daunting task for the newcomer.

Breeders

Anyone can claim to be a Rottweiler breeder. That in itself does not make the person responsible or reputable. Breeding purebred dogs is a labor of love, as well as an art and a science. Reputable breeders are educated and conscientious and care about the welfare of their dogs and the breed. They study pedigrees, plan litters, and breed only to maintain or improve the quality of the Rottweiler breed. They recognize that each breeding must be undertaken with great care and forethought. They know all the distinguishing features of their dogs' bloodlines, including temperament, and physical and mental developmental patterns.

Reputable breeders tend to have their breeding stock tested for genetic problems and will only breed those dogs who are proven clear of problems. Good breeders handle their puppies regularly and affectionately and socialize them to everything the puppies are likely to encounter as adult dogs. Most breeders perform puppy aptitude tests, or some other form of evaluation, to assess a puppy's training requirements, competitive potential, and placement options.

They can answer questions regarding the training, grooming, feeding, handling, and showing of Rottweilers, and dogs in general. They only sell their dogs to people who have passed screening questions and, in their opinion, meet the qualifications necessary to provide a permanent, first-class home for their Rottweilers.

Purchasing a Rottweiler from a reputable and responsible breeder goes well beyond the sales transaction. A good breeder will be there to help you through the transition periods, offer training advice, and help you make serious decisions regarding the care and well being of your Rottweiler. If, for some reason, your particular Rottweiler does not work out, a reputable breeder is often in a position to either take back the dog, help place it, or offer an appropriate solution.

Choosing a reputable breeder allows you to meet the mother of your puppy, which is a good way to gauge a puppy's temperament.

Backyard Breeders

Not all who call themselves breeders are working for the betterment of Rottweilers. There are those who breed dogs with little regard or concern for their dogs' ancestral background or the finer points of the Rottweiler breed. They are not necessarily bad people, and they do not always have bad intentions. Some of them truly love their dogs and provide good care. However, most are unaware of the pet overpopulation problem and do not realize they are part of the problem.

These "backyard breeders" seldom have knowledge of pedigrees, genetic disorders, or the importance of socializing puppies. Normally, they are

A good breeder will ask you questions, so that they can place their dogs in the best possible homes.

A good breeder will ask you questions, so that they can place their dogs in the best possible homes.

not involved in the sport of dogs, nor do they invest the time, money, or energy into producing dogs of sound health and temperament. They are not likely to test their breeding stock or puppies for genetic diseases. Their breeding stock is generally not breed quality, meaning it does not meet or exceed the Rottweiler breed standard for health, temperament, or appearance. Puppies are generally sold on a first-come, first-serve basis with little regard for the future welfare or living conditions of the dogs. The dogs are seldom socialized properly, and a backyard breeder is likely to be of no future help to a puppy buyer if and when things begin to go wrong.

Purchasing a Rottweiler from a backyard breeder is a gamble. You may pay less up front for a dog, but it is highly likely that you will pay a good deal more in vet bills—especially if the dog has serious health or temperament problems.

Finding a Breeder

- Your local breed club or the American Rottweiler Club (ARC) is a good place to start. They can refer you to reputable breeders, provide information on the history of the breed, its characteristics, and other useful facts.
- Veterinarians usually are familiar with local breeders, the health of their dogs, and the level of care they provide to their dogs. They usually can provide you with a list of local Rottweiler breeders.
- Dog shows are a must-do when searching for a Rottweiler. Dog shows allow you to see and compare the quality of many

Rottweilers under one roof. If possible, try to watch them in multiple venues, such as conformation, obedience, and agility. You can find information about dog shows from Infodog.com or from national registries, such as the American Kennel Club, the Kennel Club, United Kennel Club, and Canadian Kennel Club.

• Introduce yourself to the exhibitors, many of whom are also breeders. Provided they are not about to go in the ring, they normally are receptive to answering questions and providing information.

• If you feel a special connection to a breeder, ask to make an appointment to view their facility, which is usually in their home, and to meet their Rottweilers. The best indicator of temperament is the sire and dam.

Questions to Ask the Breeder

It is important that you educate yourself about the Rottweiler breed in general before visiting breeders. A basic understanding of the breed's temperament, genetic diseases, exercise requirements, and so forth, will allow you to ask informed questions. It will also help you to recognize and separate the experienced and knowledgeable breeder from the novice or backyard breeder. At the minimum, you will want to know:

When you purchase a purebred Rottweiler, you are entitled to certain types of paperwork, including a bill of sale and a pedigree.

• How long have they been involved with Rottweilers and the sport of dogs? Look for a breeder that has longevity in the breed. Generally, hobby breeders spend about 5 to 7 years breeding dogs before jumping ship to another breed, or getting out of dogs all together.

• Are the dogs registered? (This alone does not guarantee quality.)

• Do they belong to any local or national clubs/ organizations?

• Do they compete in obedience, agility, tracking, Schutzhund, etc?

• What have they accomplished with their dogs? What titles have they earned?

• Will they supply a three-generation pedigree and/or health certificate?

• Are they willing to take the dog back if things do not work out? Will they provide a full or partial refund?

• Will they give you written instructions about feeding and caring for the puppy?

- Will they be available if problems arise?
- Have the puppies eyes been examined by a canine ophthalmologist? Have they been dewormed? Vaccinated? And will the breeder supply copies of this documentation?
- Have the sire and dam been tested for genetic problems (i.e., hip dysplasia, cataracts)? Will they supply you with copies of this documentation?
- How many litters do they breed yearly? Most responsible breeders produce one, two, or maybe three litters a year. Anything more may indicate a puppy mill or backyard breeder.
- Do they have references (people you can speak with who have purchased puppies from this breeder)?

Rescue Organizations

Rescuing a purebred Rottweiler is a viable option for many prospective owners. The ARC and the Rottweiler Rescue Foundation work tirelessly with a number of rescue groups across the country to educate the public, as well as provide financial grants to rescue organizations that rescue, rehabilitate, and place purebred Rottweilers in loving, permanent homes.

Rottweilers find their way into rescue organizations for a variety of reasons including behavior problems that many owners are unprepared to deal with, such as barking, digging, chewing, or urinating in the house.

Many wonderful Rottweilers are given away or abandoned because of their owners' ignorance, indifference, or lack of compassion. Some Rottweilers in rescue have been abused or mishandled. Many lack proper socialization skills. Others have been accidentally lost or voluntarily relinquished to animal shelters or rescue groups by their owner or their owners' family because of personal illness, death, or other changes in circumstances. Pregnant bitches or young puppies occasionally find their way into rescue, but the majority of Rottweilers are older dogs, over 1 year of age.

All Rottweilers in rescue are evaluated carefully, through temperament testing, and then placed in experienced foster homes where they receive veterinary attention, obedience training,

What a Breeder Will Ask You

Reputable breeders go to great lengths to place their dogs in the best possible homes. They will want to know about you, your family, and the environment in which the Rottweiler will be raised. This information helps them to match the right puppy with the right owners. For example, a quiet, single adult who prefers watching television to outdoor activities will need a puppy with a different personality than the high-energy family with three kids who jog, hike, and ride bikes. Therefore, you should be prepared—and not offended—when you encounter breeders who are more tenacious than IRS auditors. A sampling of the many questions a breeder is likely to ask include:

- What is your knowledge of the Rottweiler breed—and dogs in general?
- Why do you want a Rottweiler?
- Have you ever trained a dog before? What breed?
- Do you currently own a Rottweiler or any other breed of dog? Or other animals including cats, horses, goats?
- What happened to your previous dog? Did he happily grow old? Was he released to a shelter? Did he escape your yard, never to be seen again?
- Will this dog be an indoor dog? Outdoor dog? Or a combination of the two?
- Do you have children? How many—and their ages?
- Are you active and energetic? Are you a workaholic who clocks 12-hour days?
- Are you assertive? Gregarious? Outgoing? Calm? Quiet? Timid?
- Do you live in a house? Apartment? The city? Country? Do you rent or own a home?
- Is your yard fenced?

socialization, grooming, and loads of TLC until they can be placed in a permanent, loving, and devoted home. These dogs will make wonderful, loving companions when coupled with the right person or family.

Purebred Rottweilers who are adopted from rescue organizations are eligible to apply for an Indefinite Listing Privilege (ILP), which allows the owners of rescued purebreds to participate in AKC companion events including obedience, agility, and tracking.

Shelters

Rottweilers of all ages find their way into humane societies for any number of reasons. Some are surrendered or abandoned by their owners. Others living in abusive conditions are confiscated by animal control officers and turned over to shelters. Lost or stray Rottweilers often are taken to a shelter by caring and compassionate residents. Many of these dogs are young to middle-aged. However, it is not unusual for older Rottweilers, some 7, 8, or 9 years old, to end up in an animal shelter. These dogs are screened by shelter personnel before becoming eligible for adoption.

THE PAPER TRAIL

When you purchase a purebred Rottweiler, you are entitled to certain types of paperwork. At the very least, you should receive a bill of sale and a pedigree. Other paperwork can include the registration certificate, health certificate, and sales contract.

Bill of Sale

You should receive a bill of sale in the form of a registration application or a signed statement that you own the dog. A bill of sale usually will include the puppy's name, sex, color, date whelped, and the name of the puppy's sire and dam. It should include the date of sale, your name, address, and telephone number.

The Pedigree

A pedigree is your Rottweiler's family tree—a genetic blueprint that authenticates your dog's ancestry. However, it does not guarantee that your Rottweiler has the genetic components that his pedigree might promise, including whether he is of show quality or free of inherited diseases or disorders. If you buy from a breeder, at the minimum, they should supply you with a three-generation pedigree. This will tell you your Rottweiler's parents, grandparents, and great-grandparents.

Registration Certificate

When a breeder registers a litter of puppies, they complete an AKC Litter Application. The form requires basic information, such as the date of birth, number of males and females born, and the registered names and numbers of the sire and dam. Once this information is sent to the AKC, with applicable fees, the AKC sends the breeder a litter kit, which includes an Individual Registration Application for each puppy in the litter.

Health Records

When it comes to dogs, the one guarantee is that there are no guarantees about health or genetic problems. Genetics is a game of chance, like flipping a coin or rolling the dice. Reputable breeders do their best to eliminate genetic problems by having breeding stock tested for genetic problems and diseases, and they will only breed those dogs who are proven clear of problems. However, they cannot guarantee with absolute certainty that a dog will not develop a specific fault or disease. The best they can do is supply you with certifications for your dog's sire and dam. This includes complete eye examinations by a canine ophthalmologist and certification from the Canine Eye Registration Foundation (CERF); hip radiographs and certification by the Orthopedic Foundation for Animals (OFA) or the University of Pennsylvania Hip Improvement Program (PennHIP); and elbow radiographs and certification from the OFA. Some breeders also may provide cardiac clearance documentation from a board-certified canine cardiologist. You also should receive a record of your Rottweiler's inoculations and worming schedule and any veterinary treatment.

Sales Contract

We've all heard the saying, "Get it in writing!" When it comes to buying and selling puppies, memories are short, information is misinterpreted, and long-term friendships can be irreparably broken. Contracts may be different for pet and show quality dogs. Sales contracts generally contain specific information including whether the dog is being sold outright or on a co-ownership basis, and a clause that gives the breeder (or seller) first right of refusal should the buyer no longer want the dog. If the puppy is sold as a show prospect, the contract may include breeder terms, which can include show rights, stud rights on a male, or puppies back from a female.

PREPARING YOUR HOME

Once you have made your selection, be it male or female, puppy or adult, pet or show dog—your life is about to be transformed. Fasten your seatbelt, and be prepared for the time of your life!

To make the transition as smooth as possible, you should do certain things before bringing your new Rottweiler home. Much of this information is geared toward preparing your home for a new puppy, but these tips apply equally to an adult dog. It is worth mentioning that when you obtain an adult dog whose background and training are a bit sketchy, such as a rescue dog, it is always a good idea to assume the dog has no training and begin his training as if he were a puppy.

Puppy Proofing

It is best to puppy-proof your house before your four-legged friend arrives. This includes removing or putting out of reach

Registering in the UK

In England, the complete registration of a litter with the KC is the responsibility of the breeder. During this process, the breeder will also officially name all the puppies. Each buyer is provided with a registration certificate for the puppy, complete with a section for the transfer of ownership that should be returned to the KC after the sale. A buyer should make sure that the breeder has signed this section of the document before completing the sale.

anything your puppy is likely to seek out and destroy. Like toddlers, puppies will explore their surroundings and try to put everything in their mouth—whether it fits or not. Your puppy is too young to understand that your expensive Italian loafers are not for teething. Pick up shoes, books, magazines, and pillows. Put up any houseplants, prescription bottles, waste baskets, and candy dishes. Tuck electrical cords behind furniture or tape them to the baseboards. Many objects, such as shoelaces, buttons, socks, marbles, paperclips, and disembowelled dolls, if swallowed, can cause life-threatening intestinal blockage and maybe require surgery to remove.

You also must puppy-proof your yard, garden, and outdoor areas. This includes picking up, removing, or fencing off hoses, sprinklers, poisonous plants, and lawn ornaments that your puppy is likely to consume when left unsupervised. Be sure to store containers of poisonous products—antifreeze, fertilizers, herbicides, and the like—on shelves and out of reach from inquisitive, thrill-seeking Rottweilers.

Make sure no gaps or holes exist in fencing to make secret passageways in your garden that a Rottweiler is likely to escape through. If your property is not fenced, be sure that your puppy is leashed each and every time he goes outdoors. He does not have the mental wherewithal to understand that the street is a dangerous place to be. It is your job to keep him safe.

SUPPLIES FOR YOUR ROTTWEILER

You will need some basic essentials, including a leash, collar, food, food and water bowls, crate, dog bed, ID tag, and an assortment of training toys and chew toys.

Beds

Your Rottweiler puppy will need a bed of his own, but it is best to hold off on anything too expensive until he is well through the chewing stage. A tenacious chewer can turn a posh canine bed into worthless confetti in the few minutes it takes you to answer the telephone. A large blanket or towel folded over several times or a cozy fleece pad placed in his crate or exercise pen will do the job for the first few months. They are easily cleaned in the washing machine and therefore less likely to develop that distinctive doggie smell.

The Right Fit

A buckle collar should be neither too tight nor too loose. Ideally, it should fit snugly around your dog's neck with enough room to fit two fingers between his neck and the collar. It should not be so tight as to restrict his breathing or cause coughing. Nor should it be so loose that it slips over his head. When too loose, the collar can easily snag on objects, such as a shrub, fence post, or another dog's tooth or paw, causing the dog to panic and inadvertently hang himself. Equally important, growing puppies quickly outgrow their collars. Be sure to check the collar size frequently on puppies. Left unchecked, a collar can become imbedded in a dog's neck, causing serious health issues. Check your dog's collar regularly to ensure that it is not frayed or worn. You don't want it to snap at an inopportune time!

Collars

Choosing a collar for your Rottweiler should not present too many challenges. There are many different types and styles from which to choose, and they are generally made of leather, nylon, cotton, or hemp. They also come in a variety of styles: buckle, harness, head halter, half-check, greyhound, choke chain, and martingale.

Every Rottweiler should wear a flat, lightweight nylon or leather buckle collar with proper identification attached. This is his ticket home should he become lost or separated from you. Nylon collars work well with puppies, because you will need to replace them several times before they are full grown. Nylon collars are relatively inexpensive and available at retail pet stores.

Leather collars are more expensive than nylon but well worth the investment for adult dogs, because they are softer yet sturdier and, given the right care, they will last a lifetime. The quality of leather collars varies considerably, so if this is your preference, be sure to select a high-quality leather collar from a reputable manufacturer.

Several types of collars work by putting pressure on your dog's neck and throat, like choke chains, prong collars, and martingale collars. While it may be tempting to use these devices on a strong dog like a Rottweiler, these collars are best left to professionals. In the hands of an inexperienced person, these types of collars can cause serious damage to a dog's throat. Taking the time to train your dog to walk properly and not pull without these devices will be much more rewarding to you both.

If you have a Rottweiler who is a nuisance puller and your best training efforts have not succeeded, you might consider a head halter—depending on your level of patience. A head halter goes over your dog's face and applies pressure to the back of the neck

Keeping Your Rottie Safe

Your Rottweiler will need a safe, contained area where he can be confined during those times when you are unable to watch him like a hawk and prevent him from getting into mischief. Most owners find a section of the kitchen makes an excellent makeshift puppy nursery. These areas generally have vinyl or washable surfaces that can easily be cleaned and disinfected, and they are normally an area of family interaction. An exercise pen or crate will help to keep your Rottweiler confined to a specific area. It is never wise to allow your puppy unsupervised or free access to your house until he is reliably housetrained and well beyond the puppy chewing stage.

rather than the front of the throat. While they can be very effective, most dogs are not used to this type of configuration, and it can require a great deal of preconditioning, patience, and diligence to make it a positive experience for your Rottweiler.

Some owners choose a harness for their dog. Keep in mind a harness will not keep your Rottweiler from pulling, but it will take the pressure off his trachea. A variety of models are available in different shapes, sizes, and materials. It is best to seek professional advice to correctly fit your Rottweiler with a harness and prevent chafing.

Crate

If you own a Rottweiler, a crate is an absolute necessity. Crates come in different shapes, sizes, and materials, each of which offers its own advantages. Folding wire crates provide good air circulation and help keep dogs cool when temperatures begin to rise. A variety of crate covers can turn any wire crate into a secure den and provide protection from the elements. Other crate types include heavy-duty, high-impact fiberglass kennels, some of which meet domestic and international requirements for airline travel; and fold-away plastic crates that are great for travel and fold away for convenient storage.

When shopping for a crate, you will want to purchase one that is big enough for your Rottweiler when he is full grown. Ideally, it should be big enough for your adult Rottweiler to stand up, turn around, and stretch out while lying down. If the crate is too big, it defeats the purpose of providing the security of a den. If it is too small, your Rottweiler will be cramped and uncomfortable, and this is neither fair nor humane. During the housetraining stage, a crate that is too large allows a puppy to use one end for sleeping and the other end as a bathroom, which defeats the crate's usefulness as a housetraining tool. Some crates come equipped with a divider panel that allows you to adjust the crate space accordingly. This option allows you to block off a portion of the crate for housetraining purposes, and this kind of crate can take your Rottweiler from the puppy stage through housetraining and into adulthood without the expense of purchasing multiple size crates. A good-quality crate will last a lifetime, and the benefits definitely make it well worth the cost when one considers the alternative of replacing damaged carpet and furniture 6 months down the road.

Exercise Pen

Like a crate, an exercise pen is indispensable for raising a well-behaved puppy. They are ideal for placing anywhere you need a temporary kennel area, such as the kitchen or family room. It can help safely confine your Rottweiler when you cannot give him your undivided attention (like when you are eating, working on the computer, or doing laundry).

If you place the exercise pen in the kitchen area—or wherever your family tends to congregate—your puppy can get used to the many sights, sounds, and smells of home from the safety of his exercise pen. Most owners prefer the kitchen area, because kitchens tend to have washable floors and can easily be cleaned and disinfected if your puppy has an accident.

Storing Dog Food

We all know how important it is to feed a high-quality pet food and most premium dry foods fit the bill. They are convenient to feed, but storing large bags of food can be a bit of a challenge, because the food is attractive not only to enterprising Rottweilers but to bugs, mice, roaches, raccoons, and any number of hungry critters.

In addition to critters, the major sources of damage to dog foods are oxygen, heat, humidity, and light. Foods with natural preservatives may have a shorter shelf life because natural preservatives, such as vitamin E, tend to break down more quickly than do artificial preservatives. Dry foods usually have a shelf life of 1 year, and canned foods are normally good for 2 years, but be sure to check the "best if used by" date on the bag or can.

The proper storage of foods can help maximize the food's shelf life and eliminate exposure to most environmental factors, including other animals. Ideally, to preserve freshness, you should store opened bags of food in a container with a tight fitting lid that minimizes the food's exposure to environmental factors. Plastic or rubber-type bins work good, but be certain to purchase bins intended specifically for storing food. If possible, keep dry food in its original bag, placing the opened bag inside the container. Store both dry and canned foods at room temperature, and never above 90°F (32°C). Storing foods below 50°F (10°C) may change the consistency and palatability of the food, but should not alter the nutritional value. Moisture encourages the growth of mold, so avoid storing dry foods in basements and bathrooms. Once opened, canned foods should be covered with a tight-fitting lid, refrigerated, and used within 3 days.

Every Rottweiler should wear a flat, lightweight nylon or leather buckle collar with proper identification attached.

Food Dishes

Your dog might consider these the most important on your list of supplies for him. After all, mealtimes are some of a dog's best times, and you will want to be sure your puppy or dog has bowls for both food and water.

Like other doggy essentials, there are plenty of bowls to choose from, and you can have a lot of fun with the selection. Keep these things in mind to make everyone's lives healthier and easier. The bowls you select should:

- Be easy to clean
- Not slip when they are placed on the floor
- Be made of material that is not potentially harmful

To meet these criteria, you should focus on stainless steel or heavy ceramic bowls—so long as the ceramic is finished with nontoxic glaze. Stainless steel is especially easy to clean, and most models come with rubberized bottoms to keep them from sliding.

As mentioned, you will need two bowls: one for water and one for food. You must have a bowl of clean, fresh water available for your Rottweiler at all times. Rinse the bowl and refill it several times a day, and thoroughly clean it as least once a day. Your dog's food bowl should be cleaned before and after his regular meals.

Identification Tags and Microchipping

All dogs should have an I.D. tag that includes his name and your telephone number. They are relatively inexpensive and well worth the investment, because they are your Rottweiler's ticket home should he become lost. Tags are readily available at retail pet outlets, mail order catalogs, and online vendors. They come in a variety of shapes, sizes, colors, and materials, and easily attach to your dog's buckle collar with an S clip or good-quality split ring. You can even find nameplates that attach directly to your dog's collar, which eliminate the unmistakable, not to mention frequently annoying, jingling noise produced by multiple tags dangling from a dog's collar.

Until recently, tattooing was the most widely used method of permanently identifying an animal. New technology has given dog owners peace of mind in the form of a microchip. It is a silicon chip, also called a transponder, about the size of a grain of rice that is painlessly inserted under your dog's skin. The microchip contains an unalterable identification number that is recorded on a central database along with your name, address, and telephone number. The microchip is scanned and the identification number is read via a hand-held electronic scanner. A universal scanner can detect and read the numbers of all major brands of microchips. A microchip will not do your Rottweiler any good if it is not registered. Several state and national registries are available for registering and storing your contact information.

Leashes

Like collars, leashes are an essential piece of equipment for any dog owner. They come in a variety of choices but, when all is said and done, choosing a leash is usually a matter of personal preference. Nylon leashes are lightweight and relatively inexpensive, and it never hurts to have an extra one in the car, motor home, or around the house. They come in every color of the rainbow and can even be personalized with your name and telephone number. They work great for smaller dogs and young puppies, but are not always the best choice for big dogs because they are hard on your hands and can slice your fingers to the bone should your dog lunge or give a good pull.

Leather leashes are quite a bit more costly but often worth the investment when you own a Rottweiler. Unlike nylon leashes, leather leashes are kinder and gentler on your hands. The more you use it, the softer and more pliable it becomes. A good quality, well cared for leather leash will be around long after your Rottweiler has settled into his golden years.

When purchasing any leash, be sure to buy one that is appropriate for the size of your dog. A lightweight nylon leash suitable for an adult Bichon Frise may work temporarily on a Rottweiler puppy, but it will do you no good on an adult dog. Generally, a ¾- or 1-inch (2 or 2.5 cm) wide leather or nylon leash will provide sufficient strength and control as your dog grows bigger and stronger.

Retractable leads are designed to extend and retract

at the touch of a button. They allow you to give your Rottweiler plenty of distance on walks without carrying a long line that can get tangled, dragged through the mud, or wrapped around bushes. A retractable lead that extends to 16 feet (5 m) allows your Rottweiler plenty of privacy to do his business or explore an open field while you lag behind. A single-finger brake button allows you to stop your dog at any time. Retractable leads also are ideal for teaching and reinforcing the Come command. If you go this route, be sure to invest in a good-quality retractable lead designed specifically for big, strong dogs; the proper lead should last a lifetime.

Toys

Rottweilers, like all dogs, not only enjoy chewing, they need to chew—especially puppies, who will experience teething pains as their baby teeth erupt and fall out. Again, a vast and endlessly entertaining selection of dog toys is available, and you and your Rottweiler can have a lot of fun selecting favorites. Your healthiest and most long-lasting selections, however, will be toys made for your Rottweiler's body type and chewing power. Hard nylon bones like Nylabones and rubber toys are made for real gnawing and gnashing. They exercise your dog's teeth and gums, promoting oral health while relieving the need to chew.

Be careful with plush toys that contain squeakers or noise-makers. Some Rottweilers will chew right through the material and may swallow the squeaker, which could become lodged in the throat.

Many kinds of edible chews and toys for dogs now provide nutritional enhancement or breath fresheners. Most are strong enough for your Rottweiler to get a good chew out of before breaking into bits that can be eaten. These should not be substitutes for the more long-lasting chew toys, but they make an enjoyable break for your dog.

TRAVELING WITH YOUR ROTTWEILER

Rottweilers are always up for fun, especially if the agenda includes spending time with their owners or accompanying them on vacation. Most Rottweilers are adaptable and make wonderful travelers, but do not wait until you are on the road to discover yours is not! Ideally, it is best to accustom your Rottweiler to traveling while he is young and more receptive to new adventures.

In the Car

For some dogs, however, riding in a car can produce a great deal of anxiety. They frequently will drool, shake, and even vomit. For dogs who have true motion sickness, which is normally associated with an inner ear problem, medications are available and can be used with the supervision of a veterinarian.

For most dogs, carsickness usually is associated with fear or an apprehension of the car noise and movement, a response to the dog's inability to control his circumstances, or a traumatic experience in a car or at the journey's end. For instance, if your puppy's first car trip was to the veterinarian's for an unpleasant shot, he may associate future rides with equally unpleasant experiences.

Provide your Rottweiler with plenty of appropriate chew toys.

If your dog has problems riding in the car, you may want to begin reconditioning him by simply sitting in the car without the motor running, while you verbally praise him for being brave and reward him with tasty treats. When he shows signs of improving, sit in the car with the motor running while you verbally praise and reward him with yummy tidbits. Then begin with short, fun, and up-beat trips around the block, to the post office, bank, and so forth. Each time, gradually increase the distance, always making the experience fun and positive. You can put a favorite blanket, toy, or treat in his crate to keep him comfy and occupied.

Dogs make excellent traveling companions, so it is well worth the training to help your dog overcome his fear of riding in a car. Doing

Did You Know?

A variety of soft canvas and water-resistant-type crates are ideal for home and travel. They are easy to set up and take down and, as an added bonus, often are machine washable. Some come equipped with extra features, such as zippered sides, storage pockets, carry bags, and wheels.

so will allow you and your dog to enjoy years of fun and travel. It is worth noting that traveling with a Rottweiler is not unlike traveling with a small child. You will need to make frequent pit stops to allow him to relieve himself, stretch his legs, and burn off a bit of pent-up energy.

If necessary, several over-the-counter products are available to help calm your Rottweiler. In severe cases, your veterinarian can prescribe a stronger, anti-anxiety medication. Always consult a veterinarian before giving your Rottweiler tranquilizers, aspirins, or medication prescribed for humans.

By Air

Dogs traveling by air are protected by U.S. Department of Agriculture (USDA) regulations. That in itself does not guarantee that your pet will be safe flying the friendly skies. However, safety regulations and precautions help minimize potential dangers, including the following:

- Dogs must be at least 8 weeks old and be weaned prior to traveling.
- Dogs must travel in airline-approved crates that meet stringent USDA regulations for size, strength, sanitation, and ventilation. Your Rottweiler may be refused a boarding pass if his kennel does not meet the government's requirements.
- A licensed veterinarian must examine your dog and issue a health certificate within 10 days of traveling.
- Dogs flying outside the continental United States may be subjected to quarantine regulations.

Regulations vary from airline to airline, so it is important to always plan ahead. Not all airlines accept dogs, and many limit the number of dogs accepted on each flight. Call the airlines well in advance of your travel plans to schedule flights. Ideally, when booking a flight try to:

- Book nonstop flights during the middle of the week, avoiding holiday or weekend travel.
- If possible, make as few layovers and plane changes as possible.
- During warm weather, choose flights early in the morning or late in the evening.
- In cooler months, choose midday flights.

Specific regulations for national and international air travel are available on the USDA web page at www.aphis.usda.gov/ac.

Hotel or Motel

If your travels with your dog include staying at a hotel or motel, call ahead to be sure they accept dogs. Not all hotels and motels accept dogs—even well-behaved Rottweilers. Some facilities allow dogs in the rooms, but they may require the dog be crated. Some larger hotels provide kennel facilities. Many require a refundable pet deposit or a nonrefundable pet fee.

To help ensure that dogs will continue to be welcomed in the future, it is important that you remain a good ambassador for the breed by following hotel and motel rules, including never leaving an unattended dog in the room. An otherwise calm dog may become anxious in unfamiliar surroundings. He may chew, urinate, defecate, or annoy other visitors with his barking. If you plan to have your Rottweiler sleep on the bed, bring an extra sheet or blanket from home to cover and protect the motel's bedspread. Without exception, always clean up after your Rottweiler and deposit any messes in designated trash receptacles.

Auto clubs usually list approved lodgings that accept dogs, and a number of guidebooks list regional and national dog-friendly motels and hotels.

Campgrounds

Like hotels and motels, not all public or private parks and campgrounds allow dogs. Most recreational vehicle clubs provide directories that include a park's pet policy. However, these policies are subject to change, so it is highly advisable to call ahead. Be sure to follow park rules, and do not allow your Rottweiler to intrude on other campers or their animals. It is never wise to leave your Rottweiler unattended or tied out where he can be teased, stolen, or attacked by another dog or wild animals.

Travel Tips

Now that you're ready to head out on a fun adventure with your Rottweiler, keep these travel safety tips in mind:

- Pack enough of your dog's regular food

If you plan ahead and do a little research, it can be easy to bring your Rottweiler with you on vacation.

and water to last the duration of the trip—and perhaps a day or two longer in case of unexpected delays. A sudden change in food or water can cause your dog to suffer from upset stomach or diarrhea. Purchase bottled water, if necessary.

- Unless your Rottweiler is a seasoned traveler, it is best to limit his food intake 2 hours before traveling. Feed the bulk of his food after you have stopped for the day.
- Never allow your Rottweiler to travel in the open bed of a pick up or with his head hanging out an open window. Dust, debris, and bugs are an ever-present danger and can damage his eyes and nostrils. A sudden, unexpected stop could throw him from the car, causing serious injury or death.
- Be careful that your Rottweiler does not overheat. Use a window shield to keep the sun from beating through the window on him, and never, ever leave him in the car unattended during warm weather.
- Walk your Rottweiler in areas designated for pets. Pick up after your dog and deposit his waste in the nearest trash bin.
- Do not permit your Rottweiler to run free, bark incessantly, or disturb other travelers.

WHEN YOU CAN'T TAKE YOUR ROTTWEILER WITH YOU

There are countless reasons your precious pooch might be excluded from your travel plans: unexpected business trips and family emergencies may arise. Or, you might be flying a significant distance. Or, the weather may be too hot or too cold for your Rottweiler. Whatever the reason, occasions may arise when you need to leave your Rottweiler for a few days or a few weeks.

Several options are available to give you peace of mind when leaving your Rottweiler behind.

Boarding Facilities

Boarding facilities have come a long way in the last 10 or 15 years. Many are now designed with the discriminating pet owner in mind, and they provide a variety of services in addition to boarding including training, daily exercise, and grooming.

Your Rottweiler's physical safety and emotional well being are paramount. Here are some tips for reducing yours and your Rottweiler's stress by choosing the best facility:

- Visit and tour the entire facility. A clean and inviting reception area does not guarantee clean kennel runs. If the proprietors do not want you touring the facility—hightail it to the nearest exit.
- Check the cleanliness of the kennels, runs, and exercise areas. Are they free of debris, excrement? How often are the kennels cleaned? How are they cleaned and disinfected between boarders? Does the kennel or exercise area smell?
- Check the security of the facility. Is it completely fenced? Do the kennels and exercise yards have good latches? Are the fences sturdy and at least 6 feet (1.9 m) high?
- Where will your Rottweiler be boarded? Indoors? Outdoors? Or a combination of the two? Are the indoor facilities heated? Are the outdoor facilities protected from the weather?
- If you have several Rottweilers, can you kennel them together? Is there an additional cost to do so?
- How frequently will your Rottweiler be walked or exercised? For how long? What type of exercise? Does someone interact or play with him? Or is he simply left unattended in an exercise yard with or without other dogs?
- Will your Rottweiler be housed with other dogs? This can be extremely dangerous and stressful to your Rottweiler, especially if the combination is not compatible. A young dog may be bullied or roughed up by an older dog, aggressive, overexcited, or rambunctious kennelmate.
- Is there a veterinarian or 24-hour emergency clinic nearby?
- What are their admission and pick-up hours? What happens if your return is delayed?
- What vaccinations are required?

Once you have decided on a facility, remember to book early.

Finding a Pet Sitter

To search for a pet sitter in your area, check with Pet Sitters International (www.petsit.com) or National Association of Professional Pet Sitters (www.petsitters.org).

Many facilities are booked months in advance, especially during the holidays. Always leave special pet-care instructions, your itinerary, and numbers to contact you or a trusted friend or relative in the event of an emergency.

Pet Sitters

If the mere thought of boarding your Rottweiler is enough to break your heart and your Rottweiler's, you might want to consider a pet sitter. He may still be heartbroken that you are gone, but there is a good chance he will be less stressed in the comfort of his own home, surrounded by his prized possessions. Most likely, he will be happier sticking to his normal routine, or as close to normal as possible, eating his regular diet, sleeping in his own bed, playing with his favorite toys, and lounging in his favorite spot. You may be lucky enough to have a responsible neighbor, trusted friend, or relative you can rely on to stop by several times a day but, if not, you might want to seek out the services of a professional pet sitter.

Pet sitters either stay at your home while you are gone or stop in during the day to feed, exercise, and check on your dog. Ask your dog-owning friends, local veterinarians, trainers, or groomers for a referral.

If you choose the pet sitting route:
- Have the pet sitter come to your home for an interview. Are they professional? Did they show up on time?
- How do they relate to your Rottweiler?
- How much experience do they have? Will they be able to recognize if your dog is sick or having a problem?
- If they are not staying at your house—how often will they come by? Once a day? Three times a day?
- Will they play with your Rottweiler? Talk to him? Love him?
- Are they licensed? Bonded? Insured?

Doggie Daycare

Doggie daycare is similar to pet sitting, but with a twist. Similar to daycare centers for human babies and toddlers, doggie daycare

Travel Checklist for Your Rottweiler

When traveling, do not forget to pack a few necessities for your dog:
- Your Rottweiler's current health certificate and rabies inoculation.
- Current photographs of your dog, to be used for identification should he become lost.
- An extra leash, collar, and set of ID tags.
- An adequate supply of food, water, and feeding dishes.
- A pooper-scooper, paper towels, or plastic bags for picking up after your Rottweiler.
- Medications and prescriptions.
- Chew toys, bones, tug toys, balls, and the like.
- A favorite blanket or bed.
- An adequate supply of doggie towels for quick cleanups, in the event your Rottweiler gets wet, dirty, or injured.

centers are for those owners who want their precious pooches to play, interact, romp, and tussle with other dogs while they are at work.

Daycare centers vary in their appearance, amenities, and cost. Some resemble park-like atmospheres with trees, park benches, kiddy pools, and playground equipment. Some facilities provide spa like amenities and lavish the dogs with attention, including hydro-baths, nail trims, and massages.

To find the right daycare facility for your Rottweiler, consider the following:
- Always visit and tour the facility.
- What type of services do they provide?
- What type of supervision do they have? How many dogs are assigned to each person?
- Are puppies and small dogs separated from large dogs?
- Are quiet, timid dogs separated from rambunctious, overzealous dogs?
- Do they have a place for your Rottweiler to get away from the other dogs?
- What type of training or experience do the employees have?
- Where will your Rottweiler spend his day? Indoors? Outdoors? In play groups?
- What vaccinations are required?
- Is there a veterinarian or emergency clinic nearby?

Once you have decided on a daycare facility, always leave a telephone number where you or a trusted friend or family member can be reached in the event of an emergency.

C h a p t e r

4

FEEDING
Your Rottweiler

The old adage, "You are what you eat" applies to your Rottweiler just as much as it applies to you. Feeding a complete and balanced canine diet is the first step in providing your dog with the necessary nutrients to live a happy, healthy life. That said, it is important that you not fall into the trap of believing what is good for you must also be good for your dog. Dogs and humans have different nutritional requirements, and a number of human foods can cause life-threatening medical problems for dogs.

Studies indicate that proper nutrition can help prevent disease, promote healthy skin and coat, and provide your Rottweiler with optimum health and longevity. While a trip to the pet food aisle can seem more difficult than brain surgery, feeding your four-legged friend a well-balanced diet is nothing to be afraid of: All it really requires is a basic understanding of canine nutrition and a keen observation of your Rottweiler and whether or not his diet is agreeing with him.

BASIC NUTRITION

When it comes to nutrition, all dogs are not created equal. Some dogs have allergies to certain food sources, such as beef, chicken, or fish, which can cause a wide variety of troubles. Others are sensitive or intolerant to poor-quality ingredients and grain-based diets. Some breeds, including the Rottweiler, are prone to juvenile obesity. Dogs—even those from the same litter—will develop differently.

One of the most important requirements in feeding your Rottweiler is to look at his individual nutritional needs and then feed a diet that provides the correct combination of nutrients. What works for one Rottweiler may not work for another because a dog's nutritional needs will change depending on his age, environment, housing conditions, exposure to heat or cold, overall health, and the emotional and physical demands placed upon him. A canine athlete competing in performance events, for example, will require more calories than a canine couch potato. If your Rottweiler's primary job is guarding the couch, it is likely he will not require as many calories as a full-time show or working dog. A

Food Factors

Your dog's age, size, health, activity level, and living conditions are all factors that determine what and how often he should be fed.

pregnant or lactating bitch's nutritional requirements will differ from that of a 10-year-old spayed Rottweiler.

To help your Rottweiler's complex system run efficiently, it is important to find the diet that provides the correct balance of nutrients for his individual requirements.

It is highly likely that your Rottweiler's diet will change several times over the course of his lifetime. However, the nuts and bolts of canine nutrition remain the same. There are six basic elements of nutrition: carbohydrates, fats, minerals, proteins, vitamins, and water.

Carbohydrates

Dogs are omnivorous animals, meaning they eat both animal and vegetable foods, and they get most of their energy from carbohydrates. Carbohydrates are the energy foods that fuel your Rottweiler's body. Scientific research indicates that up to 50 percent of an adult dog's diet can come from carbohydrates. They are often referred to as *protein-sparing nutrients*, because the action of carbohydrates (and fats) in providing energy allows protein to be used for its own unique roles.

Soluble carbohydrates consist mainly of starches and sugars and are easily digested. Insoluble carbohydrates, better known as fiber, resist enzymatic digestion in the small intestine. Fiber, while important to the overall process, is not an essential nutrient.

Carbohydrates are introduced in the diet primarily through vegetable matter, legumes, and cereal grains, such as rice, wheat, corn, barley, and oats. Unused carbohydrates are stored in the body as converted fat and as glycogen in the muscles and liver. In the absence of adequate carbohydrates, your Rottweiler's system is able to utilize fat and protein as a form of energy. However, protein is less efficient, because the body does not make a specialized storage form of protein as it does for fats and carbohydrates. When protein is used as an energy source—rather than to do its unique job of building muscle, regulating body functions, and so forth—the body must dismantle its valuable tissue proteins and use them for energy.

Fats

Fats and oils are the most concentrated sources of food energy in your Rottweiler's diet. Fats account for approximately 2.25 times more metabolizable energy—the amount of energy in the food that is available to the dog—than do carbohydrates or proteins. Fats play an important role in contributing to your dog's healthy skin and coat and aid in the absorption, transport, and storage of fat-soluble vitamins. Fats also increase the palatability of foods, but they contain more than twice the calories of proteins and carbohydrates. Just like your own diet, fats in your Rottweiler's diet should be regulated. Dogs seldom develop the cardiovascular problems that humans do, but consuming too much fat can result in excess calorie intake, which is not good for your Rottweiler's health or "waistline."

Minerals

Minerals do not yield sources of energy, but they are important in the overall nutritional equation, because they help regulate your Rottweiler's complex system and are crucial components in energy metabolism. Minerals are classified as macro minerals or micro minerals depending on their concentration in the body. Micro minerals, or *trace elements*, include iodine, iron, copper, cobalt, zinc, manganese, molybdenum, fluorine, and chromium, which dogs need in very small amounts. Macro minerals are needed in large quantities and include sodium, potassium, magnesium, calcium, and phosphorous.

Essential nutrients are those that your Rottweiler must obtain from food because his body cannot make them in sufficient quantity to meet physiological needs. If dogs get too much or too little of a specific mineral in their diets, it can upset the delicate balance and cause serious health problems including tissue damage, convulsions, increased heart rate, and anemia. You should never attempt to supplement minerals in your Rottweiler's diet without professional advice from a veterinarian.

Commercial diets are the most convenient foods to buy, store, and use.

Protein

Proteins are compounds of carbon, hydrogen, oxygen, and nitrogen atoms arranged into a string of amino acids—much like the pearls on a necklace. Amino acids are the building blocks of life because they build vital proteins that build strong muscles, ligaments, organs, bones, teeth, and coat. Protein also defends the body against disease, and is critical when it comes to the repair and maintenance of all the body's tissue, hormones, enzymes, electrolyte balances, and antibodies.

There are ten essential amino acids that your Rottweiler's body cannot make on its own or make in sufficient quantities. These amino acids must be obtained through his diet. To make protein, a cell must have all the needed amino acids available simultaneously because the body makes complete proteins only. If one amino acid is missing, the other amino acids cannot form a partial protein. If complete proteins are not formed, it reduces and limits the body's ability to grow and repair tissue.

Vitamins

A dog's body does not extract usable energy from vitamins, but they are essential as helpers in the metabolic processes. Vitamins are vital to your Rottweiler's health and available in food sources, but they can be easily destroyed in the cooking and processing of commercial dog foods. Certain vitamins are dependent on one another, and nearly every action in a dog's body requires the assistance of vitamins. Vitamin deficiencies and/or excesses can lead to serious health problems, such as anorexia, artery and vein degeneration, dehydration, muscle weakness, and impairment of motor control and balance.

One of the most important requirements in feeding your Rottweiler is to look at his individual nutritional needs.

Vitamins fall into two categories: water-soluble (B-complex and vitamin C) and fat-soluble (A, D, E, and K). Unlike humans, dogs can make vitamin C from glucose, so they do not need to acquire it in their diet. All other water-soluble vitamins must be replenished on a regular basis through diet. Fat-soluble vitamins are absorbed and stored in the body, which makes oversupplementation potentially dangerous. Seek your veterinarian's advice and read as much as you can before supplementing your dog's food.

Water

One seldom thinks of water as an essential nutrient. However, it is the single most important nutrient needed to sustain your four-legged friend's health. In addition to regulating your Rottweiler's body temperature, water plays an important part in supporting metabolic reactions and acts as the transportation system, so to speak, that allows blood to carry vital nutritional materials to the cells, and remove waste products from your dog's system.

The amount of water a dog needs to consume daily will vary from dog to dog depending on growth, stress, environment, activity, and age. A dog's need for water increases as he expends more energy during work, exercise, play, or training because dissipation of excess heat from a dog's body is accomplished largely by the evaporation of water through panting. If the weather is warm, the amount of water he requires will increase. If your Rottweiler eats primarily dry dog food, he will need access to fresh water to help aid in digestion.

Rather than trying to estimate your Rottweiler's daily water requirement, it is best to provide him with access to an abundant supply of fresh, cool drinking water at all times. When dogs have free access to water, they will normally drink enough to maintain the proper balance of body fluids. If you have less than desirable city water or are concerned about fluoride, chlorine, or lead in your water supply, consider a filtration system or try boiling water or purchasing bottled water for your Rottweiler.

Did You Know?

Infectious agents and diseases, such as leptospirosis, Giardia, and Escherichia. coli can be transmitted through contaminated water. To greatly reduce the risk of disease, do not allow your Rottweiler to drink from puddles, streams, or ponds, because the water could be contaminated with parasites that could make him ill.

WHAT TO FEED YOUR ROTTWEILER

When it comes to feeding your Rottweiler, many different options are available. From convenient commercial food to healthy homecooked meals, the most important thing to remember is to find a diet that works for you and your dog. Make sure you speak to your vet before making any drastic changes to your Rottweiler's diet.

Bones & Raw Food Diet (BARF)

It is not difficult to find ardent supporters on both sides of the controversial issue of whether a BARF diet is best for dogs. Ask a dozen people, and each one is sure to have a different opinion. Essentially, some owners believe that raw bones and foods are more suitable for their dog than highly processed foods because they believe drying, freezing, heating, or canning foods robs it of its nutritional components. The concept appears to stem from the desire to return to a more natural style of living and to feed a pure diet, similar to what wild dogs might have eaten long ago.

Stick With Premium Foods

There is no substitute for good nutrition. For maximum health and longevity, a dog must be properly fed and cared for throughout his life. Choosing a premium food over a bargain or generic brand food makes good nutritional and economic sense. Across the board, premium foods tend to be nutritionally complete, meaning they have all the required nutrients in balanced proportion, so that your Rottweiler is getting adequate amounts of all required nutrients. Premium foods also are developed to provide optimal nutrition for dogs during different stages of life, such as puppy, maintenance, active, and senior diets. The initial investment for a premium food is a bit higher on a per weight basis, but because they tend to be higher in digestibility and nutrient availability, less food is required per serving.

Two challenges arise with this type of diet: First, it is difficult to find a good source of healthy raw meat and bones, achieve the correct balance of nutrients—water, vitamins, minerals, protein, carbohydrates, fats—in the right amounts, and do so on a routine basis. Second, dogs who eat raw bones, particularly chicken and turkey bones, are highly susceptible to choking or damaging their stomachs. Both of these situations can be life threatening. In addition, parasites are a concern because dogs, like humans, are susceptible to internal parasites, bacteria, and food-borne illnesses caused by raw meat, poultry, eggs, and unprocessed milk.

Feeding a raw food and bones diet works for some owners. However, feeding this type of diet should be undertaken only after a great deal of research and understanding, and it is highly recommended that you work closely with a veterinarian or certified canine nutritionist.

Advantages:
- You control the ingredients
- Proponents believe dogs live longer, have healthy lives, and better immune systems

Disadvantages:
- Time consuming to prepare
- Difficult to find fresh, high-quality raw meats
- More expensive—especially if using organic foods
- Difficult to achieve complete and balanced levels of nutrients on a regular basis
- Concern of bacterial infections, parasites, and food-borne illnesses for both dogs and humans when handling and eating raw foods (*i.e., E.coli and Salmonella*)
- Choking hazards when eating raw bones

Commercial Diets

Commercial diets are undoubtedly the most convenient foods to buy, store, and use. They are readily available and, when compared to homemade diets, they are definitely less time consuming. Most major dog-food manufacturers, and a number of veterinary hospitals, have invested enormous sums of money in researching and studying the nutritional requirements of dogs in different stages of life. As a result, they are quite knowledgeable about the requirements of puppies, adult dogs, athletic dogs, pregnant bitches, and senior dogs, and what constitutes good canine nutrition.

It is also important to keep in mind that the commercial dog food industry is a multibillion-dollar-a year business. Advertising experts spend a significant amount of time researching, developing, and marketing products in a manner to convince you to buy a particular brand. This is not necessarily bad, but it is important to keep in mind if you are choosing a food because of the creative advertisements and fancy packaging, rather than nutritional requirements of your dog.

Commercial foods tend to be classified into food types: dry, canned, and semi-moist. Frozen and dehydrated foods also are becoming increasingly popular in the competitive dog food market.

Canned Foods

Canned foods are mostly water—approximately 75 percent. They contain more meat than a dry diet and little or no grain.

Advantages:
- High palatability
- Easier to digest
- Contains a higher meat protein level
- Canning process kills harmful bacteria
- Long shelf life

Disadvantages:
- More expensive than dry foods
- Provides no abrasion from chewing, which allows faster plaque and tartar build-up on teeth
- Requires refrigeration after opening
- High-heat processing can destroy some nutrients
- Due to high water content, moist foods have fewer nutrients than other foods. More food must be eaten to satisfy energy and nutrient needs.

Dehydrated Foods

Dehydrated foods, which contain fresh meats, grains, and vegetables, are dehydrated at low temperatures to preserve all the natural nutrients.

Advantages:
- Once dehydrated, foods can last indefinitely
- Easy to store

Disadvantages:
- Can be costly
- When rehydrated, the food becomes a moist mixture
- Does not provide abrasion or scarping while chewing.
- Does not satisfy a puppy's need to chew

Dry Food

Dry foods, commonly called "kibble," contain between 6 to 10 percent moisture (water) and a high percentage of carbohydrates in the form of grains. Most major brand dog food manufactures make a large-breed puppy kibble specifically formulated for the needs of growing puppies. The idea is to avoid excessive caloric intake in order to manage excessive weight gain and any subsequent skeletal problems associated with the maturation rate of large-breed dogs.

With a breed like the Rottweiler, you'll want to avoid excessive caloric intake in order to manage excessive weight gain.

Advantages:
- Economical, readily available, and convenient to buy, store, and use
- Good shelf life; does not require refrigeration
- May improve dental hygiene through chewing and grinding, which aids in the removal of dental plaque, although this is highly debatable among the experts (does not eliminate the need for regular dental care)
- Provides some exercise for a dog's mouth, and helps satisfy a puppy's need to chew
- High-quality brands have high caloric density and good digestibility, which means lower amounts per serving need to be consumed
- Stool is usually smaller and more compact.

Disadvantages:
- Less palatable to some dogs than canned or semi-moist foods
- High heats used in the processing stage can destroy valuable nutrients

Semi-moist Foods

Semi-moist foods are often shaped into patties and come in a prepackaged size convenient for feeding. They are generally marketed in sealed and resealable pouches. They are 25 to 35 percent water. Ingredients can include fresh or frozen animal tissues, cereal grains, fats, and simple sugars. It is worth noting that semi-moist foods contain propylene glycol, which is an odorless, tasteless, slightly syrupy liquid used to make antifreeze and de-icing products. Propylene glycol is generally recognized as safe by the U.S. Food and Drug Administration (FDA) for use in dog food and other animal feeds. It is used to absorb extra water and maintain moisture, and as a solvent for food coloring and flavor.

Advantages:
- High sugar content may increase palatability
- Less offensive smelling than canned foods
- Good shelf life; does not require refrigeration

Disadvantages:
- High sugar levels in dog food cause spikes in blood sugar levels and contribute to obesity
- High sugar levels may aggravate an existing or borderline diabetic condition
- Contains high levels of salt
- Contains propylene glycol
- Sticky, sugary foods can contribute to dental disease
- If left out for long periods of time, such as in a dog bowl, it will dry out reducing palatability

Homemade Diets

Let's face it, unless you are an experienced canine nutritionist with an abundance of time and energy on your hands, feeding a homemade diet is easier said than done. Preparing your Rottweiler's food from scratch is a romantic and selfless notion. After all, who does not want the best for their dog? What owner does not want to feed foods free of preservatives, additives, and who knows what else?

Truth be told, homemade diets are a time consuming, labor-intensive, expensive, and complicated process. It is tricky, albeit not impossible, to prepare a canine diet on a routine daily basis that is complete and balanced and contains the proper ratio of nutrients. Do you know the calcium/phosphorous ratio in the diet you are

Prescription Diets

Prescription diets are special-formula diets prepared by dog food manufacturers and normally available only through a licensed veterinarian. They are designed to meet the special medical needs of dogs, such as low protein and mineral diets for kidney disease; low protein, magnesium, calcium, phosphorous for bladder stones; lamb- and rice-based diets for food-induced allergies; and low-calorie foods for weight-reduction diets.

preparing? It is important stuff. The nutritional value of raw ingredients will fluctuate depending on their sources, and supplementing with vitamins and minerals is usually necessary. However, that can be harmful to your dog if too much or too little or the wrong combinations of supplements are used. If you had an unlimited budget, and were so inclined, you could mix all the food ingredients, supplements, treats, snacks, and so forth, into a blender and have the sample professionally analyzed.

The bottom line: When you choose to feed a homemade diet, you assume full responsibility for the nutritional status of your Rottweiler. If this is what you decide to do, it is prudent to consult with a veterinarian or certified veterinary nutritionist before proceeding.

Advantages:
- You control the ingredients.
- You can customize by providing a mixture of fresh meat, chicken, fish, vegetables, and commercial kibble.
- You can provide a combination of cooked and raw ingredients.

Disadvantages:
- Time consuming to prepare
- More expensive—especially if using organic ingredients
- Difficult to achieve complete and balanced levels of nutrients on a regular basis
- Concern of bacterial infections, parasites, and food-borne illnesses for both dogs and humans handling and eating raw foods (i.e., *E.coli* and *Salmonella*)

FEEDING YOUR ROTTWEILER PUPPY

A Rottweiler puppy has gigantic nutritional demands. Beside the fact that a puppy spends a significant part of his day playing, which requires a lot of calories, his body is growing rapidly. His system is building strong muscles, bones, and vital organs, and establishing a resistance to disease. As a result, for the first 12 months of his life, he needs a specially formulated growth food that is designed exclusively for his greater energy and nutritional needs.

A growing puppy needs about twice as many calories per kilogram of body weight as an adult Rottweiler. Since puppies have small stomachs, they also need to be fed smaller amounts of food three or four times a day until they are about 6 months old. From 6 months to 1 year of age and thereafter, you should feed your Rottweiler two times a day—once in the morning and again in the evening.

Growth rates and appetites of puppies are primarily dictated by genetics and will vary from puppy to puppy, so feeding the correct amount can be a bit tricky. The feeding guidelines on puppy foods are just that—guidelines. They are not etched in stone, and many dog food manufacturers tend to be overly generous with their proportions. Your veterinarian can help you determine the proper amount to feed.

For the first few days after bringing your precious pooch home, you should continue feeding the same type and brand of puppy food he has been eating, provided he has been eating a well-balanced, good-quality puppy food. Depending on where and from whom you purchase your Rottweiler, this may or may not be the case.

If you intend to switch foods, it is best to do so slowly to prevent intestinal upset. Veterinarians recommend switching foods over the course of 7 to 10 days to prevent upset stomachs, vomiting, loose stool, or constipation. To do this, make a mixture of 75 percent old food and 25 percent new food. Feed this mixture for 3 or 4 days. Then make a mixture of 50 percent old food and 50 percent new food. Feed this mixture for 3 or 4 days. Then make a mixture of 25 percent old food and 75 percent new food. Feed this mixture for 3 or 4 days. Then you can start feeding 100 percent new food.

For the first few days after bringing your Rottweiler home, you should continue feeding the same type and brand of puppy food he has been eating.

Protein and Larger-Breed Puppies

Protein is essential in all aspects of growth and development. However, not all proteins are created equal. Each protein is different in its ability to be broken down into amino acids. If a dog gets too much protein, some gets excreted in the urine, and the rest gets used as calories or is converted to fat and stored in the body.

Several studies indicate that feeding large- and giant-breed puppies diets that contain lower amounts of protein and fat may reduce the incidence of bone and joint problems that can plague larger breeds. As a result, dog food

"Large-Breed" Puppy Food

When it comes to feeding "large-breed" puppy formulas, opponents and proponents abound on both sides of the issue. Do your research, and discuss the issue with your Rottweiler's veterinarian to find the food plan right for your puppy.

manufacturers began developing and marketing foods geared specifically toward large- and giant-breed dogs. These types of puppy foods have reduced amounts of protein and fat.

Here's where it gets a bit complicated: If you do the math, the difference in protein amounts between some large-breed and regular puppy food often is negligible. Not all foods, but some. And some manufacturers use different types and qualities of protein that have varying degrees of digestibility. Therefore, owners need to be a bit savvy about reading labels and deciphering nutritional requirements, types of ingredients, and so forth.

Furthermore, most experts believe that large-breed puppy bone problems are primarily genetic and inherited. These problems are exacerbated when a puppy is overweight. The problem is not necessarily the food, but the amount of food. Too many owners overfeed their puppies, allowing them to become fat. Some owners think bigger is better, so they overfeed their puppy hoping he will grow into a big adult dog. If you overfeed any puppy, be it a miniature or a large-breed dog, a good chance exists that the puppy will get fat, which is not healthy. If you have a puppy who is predisposed to bone and joint problems, the last thing you want is for him to be overweight because that puts additional stress and strain on his little bones, joints, and ligaments.

Many experts agree that the logic of reducing fat, protein, and calcium levels when feeding large-breed puppies sounds good theoretically, but when you send it down the runway, it doesn't always fly. Much skepticism exists about whether it makes a significant difference in the incidence of bone growth problems. Most believe large-breed puppy foods are good quality and provide the optimum nutritional requirements. They also believe that feeding the appropriate amount of a good premium-quality puppy food works, too. Simply put, if cost isn't a factor, and someone can afford to feed a large-breed puppy formula, it is a good choice. However, if someone chooses to feed an affordable premium all-purpose puppy food, experts think it is a reasonable option.

Ask a dozen people and you are likely to get a dozen different answers when it comes to feeding "large-breed" puppy formulas. To further complicate the matter, some breeders recommend feeding a good-quality, all-purpose puppy food until the dog is 6 months old, then switch to a premium adult food.

Having a basic understanding of canine nutritional

Feeding Chart

Who	Puppy (up to 6 months)	Puppy (6 months to 1 year)	Adult (1 to 8 years)	Senior (1 to 8 years)
What	Specially formulated food	Specially formulated puppy food	Adult maintenance food	Adult maintenance food (lower qty) or senior food
When	3 to 4 times a day	2 times a day	2 times a day	2 times a day

requirements, understanding how to decipher dog food labels, and talking to your veterinarian are the best way to ensure your Rottweiler puppy is getting the appropriate food.

Scheduled Feeding Versus Free-Feeding

You must feed your puppy at regular times. Whatever food is left after 15 minutes, you should pick up and throw away. This regimen will help your puppy establish a regular routine of eating and eliminating, which will help speed up the housetraining process. Designated feeding times also can help with the bonding process, as well as help to avoid obesity in your puppy. Juvenile obesity increases the number of fat cells in a puppy and predisposes him to obesity for the rest of his life.

Free-feeding, which is putting the food out, leaving it all day, and allowing your puppy to eat at his leisure, is not recommended. It does not establish a set schedule for feeding and eliminating. While a few dogs are able to regulate their food intake, most dogs will eat and eat and eat as long as food is available. They eat until they make themselves sick, and then they gleefully start all over again. If food is perpetually available, some dogs will develop the annoying and potential dangerous habit of food-bowl guarding. Finally, if you have multiple dogs, you will not know for certain if your puppy is eating or the other dogs are eating for him.

FEEDING YOUR ADULT ROTTWEILER

Different breeds of dogs reach maturity at different ages. As a general rule, smaller breeds tend to reach adulthood sooner than large-breed dogs. It is highly likely that your Rottweiler will reach

Did You Know?

A supplement is anything that is given in addition to a dog's feed. It can include something as simple as adding a splash of vegetable oil, a few pieces of leftover steak, or half a cup of chicken broth to increase the palatability of your dog's food. While these tidbits are not likely to upset your Rottweiler's nutritional balances—provided they account for less than 10 percent off your dog's caloric intake—too many tasty tidbits, gravies, and other gastronomic delicacies can add unnecessary calories and result in unwanted weight gain.

adulthood around 12 months of age. That said, the age of maturity varies from Rottweiler to Rottweiler, with some Rotties reaching maturity sooner or later than others. Some Rottweiler's do not reach physical maturity until they are 2, 3, or 4 years of age.

Adult foods, often called *maintenance diets,* are specially designed foods that satisfy the energy and nutritional needs of adult dogs who have reached maturity. These diets are designed to provide the proper quantities of nutrients to support a mature Rottweiler's lifestyle. Rottweilers who are very active, under physical or emotional stress, and lactating bitches have different nutrient requirements than the average canine couch potato. Your veterinarian can help you determine when and what type of adult food to choose. Most experts recommend feeding an adult dog twice a day—once in the morning and again in the early evening. As with puppies, pick up any food left after 15 minutes and toss it.

FEEDING YOUR SENIOR ROTTWEILER

Different dogs age at different rates and determining if and when you should begin feeding a senior food will depend on your individual dog. It is impossible to arbitrarily set an old-age age. You cannot randomly say that Rottweilers are old at 7 or 8 years of age. Dogs age differently, depending on their genetics and overall lifestyle.

A good rule of thumb is to divide the average lifespan of a Rottweiler into thirds. When your Rottweiler is in the last 1/3 stage of his life, he is usually considered an older dog. Using that simplified mathematical equation, the average Rottweiler would be considered an older dog around 6 or 7 years of age. Again, exceptions exist to every rule, and some Rottweilers remain physically and cognitively young at 8 or 9 years of age.

Older dogs usually require a diet that is still complete and well balanced, yet lower in calories, protein, and fat. In some instance, you may be able to feed your Rottweiler his regular adult food but in lower quantities. Or you may need to switch to a diet designed specifically for senior dogs.

Because older dogs do not normally get as much exercise as their younger counterparts, losing weight can be difficult for them. Maintaining a sensible weight throughout your Rottweiler's entire life is one of the most important and humane things you can do to help your dog retain good health and

Foods to Die For

Dogs have different metabolisms, and some human foods (and nonfood items) can cause serious health problems, ranging from a mild upset stomach to death. Dogs should not get the final word when it comes to what is and is not good for them. After all, some will gleefully eat poop, rocks, and dirt, if you let them. The list below is a sampling of some of the most common foods that can cause your Rottweiler serious health problems if ingested. It is in your dog's best interest to keep these items from his possession. If you suspect your Rottweiler has ingested a toxic substance, do not delay. Seek veterinary attention immediately.

- Alcoholic beverages can cause intoxication, coma, and, in some instances, death.
- Bones from fish, poultry, or other meat sources can cause obstruction or laceration of the digestive system.
- Cat food, while not fatal, is high in protein and fat and particularly appetizing for enterprising Rottweilers. Too much can cause intestinal upset and unnecessary weight gain.
- Chocolate — oh, so yummy for people, but deadly for dogs. It can increase a dog's heart rate and breathing, resulting in serious illness and death.
- Grapes and raisins contain a toxin that can damage your Rottweiler's kidneys.
- Macadamia nuts contain a toxin that can affect your Rottweiler's digestive and nervous system, and muscles. A double dose of trouble is chocolate-covered macadamia nuts!
- Mushrooms can contain toxins that vary depending on the species. They affect multiple systems and result in shock and death. They grow in the wild — and your backyard. Closely supervise your dog to prevent ingestion.
- Onions and garlic contain sulfoxides and disulfides, which can be toxic to dogs. They can damage red blood cells and cause anemia.
- Tobacco contains nicotine and can cause an increased heartbeat, collapse, coma, and death.

increase the quality and length of his life. Knowing this ahead of time, you can plan ahead and take precautions that do not allow your Rottweiler to become overweight at any stage of his life.

On the other side of the spectrum, older dogs occasionally will go off of their food, meaning they lose interest in it, and they may choose to eat only once a day. If your Rottweiler is losing weight or his eating habits have changed, it is important that a veterinarian examine him to rule out any possible disease problems. Because dogs age at different rates, it is best to work closely with a veterinarian as your Rottweiler begins to enter his senior years. Your veterinarian can help you determine the specific nutritional and supplemental needs of your Rottweiler in this stage of his life.

SUPPLEMENTS

In most cases, if you are feeding a professional-quality diet that is complete and well balanced, supplementing is not recommended. Remember, your Rottweiler's system is complex and, to run efficiently, it must receive the proper amounts of nutrients in a balanced ratio. By supplementing your Rottweiler's

Preventing begging behaviors is easy if you make it a rule from day one that no one — this includes kids, spouses, in-laws, and visitors — feed the dog from the table or at any other time while they are eating.

diet, you may inadvertently upset that intricate balance. When too much of one nutrient is present and too little of another, your Rottweiler's diet is out of balance. Fat-soluble vitamins, for example, are stored in a dog's body, so it is easy to overdose with supplementation and cause nutritional imbalances.

Canine supplements are a multimillion-dollar business. Nutraceuticals are a type of supplement often called *phytochemicals* or *functional foods*. They include natural remedies, such as vitamins, botanicals, nutrients, and minerals. The most popular canine nutraceuticals are the joint-protective products—glucosamine, chondroitin, and methylsulfonylmethane (MSM)—that are typically prescribed for older dogs and are used to help diminish the symptoms of osteoarthritis—the wear-and-tear type of arthritis. They also are used to reduce injuries to joint surfaces and promote the healing of cartilage.

While nutraceuticals are popular alternatives to many of the traditional, synthesized medications, they are not without problems. For starters, they are not subject to FDA regulation and, as a result, they are poorly regulated. What the label says may not necessarily be what is in the bottle. Also, little scientific evidence confirms the benefits of nutraceuticals. What experts know about nutraceuticals and their use in the treatment of dogs is empirical. Simply put, the evidence comes less from clinical trials and more from the anecdotes and testimonials of veterinarians and dog people, such as handlers, breeders, and trainers.

It is important to note that "alternative" or "herbal" does not mean harmless. Supplements can cause side effects or result in cross-reactions if combined with other supplements or medications. To prevent problems, always consult your veterinarian before using supplements.

OBESITY

Like people, dogs who are carrying around extra pounds are subjected to serious health issues including diabetes, heart disease, increased blood pressure, and digestive disorders. They have increased surgical risks, decreased immune functions, and are more susceptible to injuries, including damage to joints, bones, and ligaments. Overweight and obese Rottweilers have a diminished quality of life, and they tend to die at a younger age than do their physically fit counterparts.

Participating in sports like agility can help keep your Rottweiler fit and trim.

As a rule, obesity in Rottweilers is not any more common or uncommon than in any other breed. Regardless of the breed, dogs who are overfed—be it too much kibble or too many table scraps and high-fat snacks—are likely to become overweight or downright obese. Some dogs, regardless of the breed, are "easy keepers"—meaning their weight seldom fluctuates. Others will gain weight with just a few extra kibbles and snacks each day.

Studies indicate that as human's become more obese, so too do their dogs. Rottweilers who are overweight as puppies are more prone to be overweight adult dogs. Juvenile obesity increases the number of fat cells in the dog's body and predisposes him to obesity for the rest of his life.

Is My Rottweiler Overweight?

A Rottweiler's weight can range from ideal to slightly overweight to downright obese—or somewhere in between. To be sure your Rottweiler is not packing extra pounds, follow these simple guidelines for assessing your Rottweiler's weight:

- *Ideally, you should be able to feel your Rottweiler's ribs,* and they should have minimal fat covering them. His tail base—the pelvic bone area near his tail—can be felt under a thin layer of fat. When viewed from the side, his abdominal tuck—the underline of his body, where his belly appears to draw up toward his hind end—should be evident. When standing over your Rottweiler and viewing him from above, his waist—the section behind his ribs—is well proportioned.

It is easier to keep the weight off than it is to take it off. If your Rottweiler is not overweight, the most thoughtful and compassionate deed you can do for him is to not allow him to gain extra pounds. Rottweilers who are overweight as young dogs are at a greater risk to become overweight adult dogs.

- *In a Rottweiler who is a few pounds overweight,* you can still feel his ribs, but they have a moderate or slight excess of fat covering them. His tail base bones can be felt under a moderate layer of fat. His abdominal tuck is still evident. His waist, when viewed from above, is visible, but not nearly as prominent as with a lean Rottweiler.
- *In a Rottweiler who is more than a few pounds overweight,* you will have difficulty feeling his ribs. A thick or heavy layer of fat will cover them. His abdominal tuck may still be present. His waist, when viewed from above, is barely visible.
- *In a very overweight Rottweiler,* you cannot feel his ribs because of the heavy layer of fat covering them. His back and hip region will have fat deposits, and his waist is nonexistent. His abdominal tuck is gone, and his belly will most likely appear distended. He may have fat deposits on his spine, chest, shoulders, neck, and legs.

Your veterinarian can help you determine the ideal weight for your Rottweiler and develop a long-term plan to condition his body and provide him a good start toward a longer, healthier life.

The Battle of the Bulge

How can you help your Rottweiler fight the battle of the bulge? If your Rottweiler is currently overweight or obese, the first step should be a trip to the veterinarian. Some medical conditions, such as hypothyroidism and Cushing's disease, can contribute to weight gain, but those cases represent a very small portion of overweight dogs, perhaps less than 5 percent, according to experts. Some medications, such as prednisone and phenobarbital, can influence a dog's metabolism and appetite. A veterinarian can examine your Rottweiler to assess his overall health and medical condition, and she can advise you on sensible and healthy ways to reduce your Rottweiler's weight.

Feeding the Right Food

To keep your Rottweiler's figure fit and trim, you must choose the food that best suits his activity level and life stage. Overweight and underweight dogs, as well as puppies, athletic, and geriatric dogs have different nutritional and caloric requirements. Puppies require specially formulated diets. An older, less active Rottweiler generally needs fewer calories than a young, energetic Rottweiler, and an overweight Rottweiler may require a special reduced-calorie diet. When in doubt, always seek veterinary assistance in choosing the food that best suits your Rottweiler. A good, well-balanced diet is a sure way to keep your Rottweiler fit, lean, and happy, and it can increase his lifespan by nearly 2 years! It is also one of the most kindhearted gifts you can give your dog.

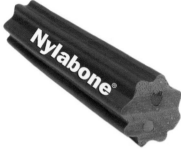

Table Scraps

If your Rottweiler is willing to bargain with the devil in exchange for a tasty tidbit from the table, you will need to grow a thick skin and ignore his woeful and pleading stares. Table scraps are one of the worst offenders when it comes to sabotaging your dog's weight-maintenance program. A tasty tidbit of steak here, a nibble of chicken there, a potato skin, a French fry or two—what's the harm, right? It is better for table scraps to go to waste than to your Rottweiler's waist. If you cannot resist feeding a tidbit of leftover steak or chicken, put it in the refrigerator and feed it at a later time as a training treat. Feeding from the table also encourages begging, which is a difficult habit to break.

Treats

James Spratt achieved fame by making dog biscuits in London during the mid-1800s. Today, some 145 years later, the number of commercial dog treats available is mind-boggling! When choosing treats, it is important to read labels carefully and choose treats that are low in fat, sugar, and salt. Small pieces of fruit or fresh veggies are good alternatives to store bought treats. Or try baking your four-legged friend some yummy, low-fat, homemade treats. Treats should be a reward for a job well done, such as coming when called. Treats should never be a substitute for well-deserved hugs and kisses.

Exercise, Exercise, Exercise

If your Rottweiler is logging too much couch time, it is time to get him moving. Exercise can do wonders for improving your Rottweiler's overall physical and mental health. Exercise not only helps to burn calories, it strengthens your dog's respiratory system, aids in digestion, and helps get oxygen to tissue cells. Exercise keeps

If you do not want your Rottweiler begging for food, you should discourage the behavior from day one. Some owners are under the mistaken impression that treating their Rottweiler to tasty tidbits of people food will make him love them more. Not so! A Rottweiler who is rewarded for begging quickly learns to manipulate you. It is a short leap from sad and sympathetic beggar to seasoned con artist.

muscles toned and joints flexible, releases boredom, and will keep your Rottweiler's mind active.

Equally important, interactive exercise can help strengthen the human–canine bond. If your Rottweiler is overweight or out of shape, start slow and progress at a rate that is within your Rottweiler's physical capabilities. If you are uncertain about the amount and method of exercise, always seek veterinary advice. A veterinarian can help you design an exercise program that is most appropriate for your Rottweiler's individual health.

OTHER FOOD-ASSOCIATED PROBLEMS

Begging

Generally speaking, it's not a good idea to allow begging from any breed—unless, of course, you and your dinner guests don't mind a dog shoving his head in your laps, drooling, pawing, and staring pathetically while you dine by candlelight. Rottweilers are bigger and more powerful than most dogs, which can make them more annoying.

It really comes down to expectations and management. How do you expect your dog to behave as he grows and matures into an adult dog? If you allow begging…where do you draw the line? What about swiping food off the kitchen counter or, heaven forbid, the supper table? If a dog thinks he can get away with begging and stealing food, what about guarding his food bowl or favorite toy? What about growling and snapping at his owners? Dogs who do not have boundaries grow into unruly hooligans. Once you've decided on your expectations, such as no begging for food, you must manage his environment so that he is not put in a position where he is allowed to develop bad habits.

Puppies should be kept away from the table while you eat, so that they are not inadvertently rewarded by dropped food. An alternative is to use a baby gate to keep your puppy corralled in another room and away from where you are eating. He will be able to see you while you eat and also get used to waiting patiently without constantly being nagged.

If your Rottweiler is well trained, you can put him on a down-stay while you eat, and then verbally praise him for being a good boy. A word of caution: It is difficult, if not impossible, for some dogs, especially young dogs, to maintain their composure while in the presence of food. It is better to restrict his access to the dinner table than to continually nag him to stop begging.

If your Rottweiler has already learned to beg, drool, or otherwise look sad and pathetic during mealtime, it is highly likely someone has been sneaking him tidbits of food. Rottweiler's are intelligent and patient! They will gladly wait and stare with sad, mournful eyes for as long as it takes to sample a delightful chunk of steak, a French fry or two, a tasty morsel of ham, or a pinch of bagel and cream cheese. If you cannot resist sharing your food, put scraps in the refrigerator and feed them at a later time as a training treat. Use the tidbits to teach your Rottweiler to down, speak, rollover—or to sit up and beg properly, as a trick! Remember, any table scraps or bits and pieces of food, even when used as training treats, should be included in your dog's daily caloric count. Otherwise, your Rottweiler is likely to put on a few extra pounds.

Teach your puppy to take food nicely from your hand.

Snatching Food

Some puppies seem to naturally take food nicely without trying to trim your cuticles or chew your fingers. Other puppies need to be taught early on not to bite the hand that feeds them—literally! It is in your Rottweiler's best interest to nip this behavior in the bud right away. Left unchecked, this behavior can get downright nasty. Keep in mind that you may inadvertently be teaching your puppy to snatch at food if you are pulling your hand away as he starts to take the food.

If your Rottweiler has already developed the annoying and painful habit of snapping or snatching food, try this approach: Hold a tasty tidbit of food in the palm of your hand and then fold your hand so that you make a fist. Offer him the back of your hand. He will be able to smell the treat, but your fingers will not be exposed or vulnerable. Most likely, he will sniff your hand trying to expose the treat. If he is gentle, open your hand and present the treat in the palm of your hand. He will be able to take the treat without nipping your fingers. As he does so, praise warmly. "Good boy!" Eventually, he will learn to wait until you have opened your hand before he gets a treat.

GROOMING
Your Rottweiler

The Rottweiler is a double-coated breed with a medium-length top coat (or outer coat) and a soft, downy undercoat that develops as the dog reaches adulthood. The top coat may appear relatively short, but that does not mean the breed needs no grooming.

Grooming your Rottweiler on a regular basis not only keeps his skin and coat in tip-top condition, but also allows you to check his entire body for lumps, bumps, cuts, rashes, dry skin, fleas, ticks, stickers, and the like. You can check his feet for cuts, torn pads, or broken nails, and examine his mouth for tartar, damaged teeth, or discolored gums. Regular grooming will improve your Rottweiler's appearance, making him the envy of the neighborhood—not to mention the most handsome specimen on the block!

Most dogs love to be groomed, and that makes the necessary chore a great way to spend quality time with your Rottweiler while simultaneously building a strong and mutually trusting human–canine relationship. Equally important, when you regularly groom your Rottweiler, you will quickly recognize when something is amiss.

If you have a Rottweiler puppy, it is a good idea to start good grooming practices right away. A puppy who is exposed to positive and delightful grooming experiences will grow into an adult dog who takes pleasure in the regular routine. Few things are as frustrating as trying to wrestle down a 100-pound (45.4 kg) Rottweiler who hates to be groomed.

GETTING YOUR ROTTWEILER USED TO GROOMING

If grooming is new to your Rottweiler, don't despair. Like anything else, it is best to start slow and progress at a rate that is suitable for the age and mental maturity of your dog.

If you have a grooming table, begin by teaching your Rottweiler to stand on the table. For a puppy, any sturdy surface, such as a bench or crate top, covered with a nonskid, nonslip surface is sufficient. Sitting or kneeling on the floor with your Rottweiler works in a pinch, too. In addition, it is prudent to have all the grooming tools out and within easy

Bath Supplies

- Shampoo designed for dogs
- Coat conditioner
- Dry towels

reach *before* you start grooming. You never want to turn your back or leave your Rottweiler on a grooming table unattended. A young Rottweiler can easily be injured should he fall or jump.

Puppies have limited attention spans, so do not expect your Rottweiler to stand still for extended periods of time. In the beginning, you want progress—not perfection. Your goal is for him to stand still for a few seconds while you praise him. Harsh handling during these learning stages will only build resentment toward the necessary chore. Progress to the point where your puppy will accept having his body stroked with your hand, then gently, slowly, and calmly brush him all over. In the beginning, your Rottweiler may be frightened, nervous, or unsure. Patience and kind handling will help to build his confidence and teach him to accept and enjoy the grooming process.

A common problem arises when owners make grooming a game, or allow the dog to make it a game. Grooming should definitely be a positive and pleasant experience, but a dog who decides grooming is a game is likely to become overstimulated and nip or bite at the hand that grooms him. It is best to stop that behavior right away, because it can become an established behavior that is difficult to break.

The Grooming Table

It's quite easy to get your puppy on and off a grooming table while you are getting him used to grooming. However, a full-grown Rottweiler is too heavy for most people to lift—but don't discard the grooming table! Teach him "feet up"—which is to put his front feet on the grooming table, then you can boost his back legs up and onto the table. (This works great for boosting large dogs into SUVs, vans, and larger cars.) Most dogs learn "feet up" when owners pat the table and say the command "feet up." When the dog puts his feet up—praise and reward. If he doesn't get the hang of "feet up," simply lift his front feet onto the table then hoist his rear legs up.

Getting off is a bit trickier. Most owners employ a lifting and jumping combination. Put one of your arms between the dog's front legs, and your other arm wrapped under the dog's chest/stomach area. As the dog jumps, your arm positioning helps guide him and cushion a hard landing. You certainly don't want him jumping off the table by himself onto concrete and hurting himself. Some companies manufacture ramps specifically for loading dogs into and out of cars, onto grooming tables, and other hard-to-reach places. If you are handy with a hammer and nails, you can make your own ramp or build a couple of stackable boxes on which he can climb up and down.

ANAL GLANDS

Dogs have glands on each side of the anus. When viewing a dog from behind, they are located at approximately the four and eight o'clock positions. The glands are emptied naturally with bowel movements. However, it is not uncommon for them to become impacted (clogged), infected, or abscessed. When the glands become full and uncomfortable, a Rottweiler may scoot along the floor, or lick the anal area excessively. Abscessed or infected glands can be very painful, and a dog may be hesitant to allow you to touch around the area.

Teach your Rottweiler to put his front feet on the grooming table, then you can boost his back legs up and onto the table.

When glands become clogged, they must be expressed, or emptied, by applying pressure to the glands. While some owners have learned to express the glands themselves, most prefer to leave it to a veterinarian. Abscessed anal glands require veterinary attention, as do some impacted or clogged glands.

BATHING

How often your Rottweiler requires bathing will depend on where you live, how much time he spends outside, and how dirty he gets. If he is your constant companion on walks, jogs, hikes, and trips to the barn or pasture, he may require bathing on a regular basis, say, every few weeks or so. If he spends a great deal of time indoors, he may require bathing once every 4 to 6 weeks. No cut-and-dried formula exists for how often your Rottweiler needs bathing. You will need to be the judge.

Most Rottweilers enjoy the water and are

quite amenable to baths. In warmer climates, you may be able to bathe your dog outdoors with a garden hose. Otherwise, a rubber mat on the bottom of a bathtub or shower stall will provide secure footing and prevent him from slipping. If you are bathing your dog indoors, have plenty of dry towels ready and be prepared to wipe down all the walls and fixtures in the bathroom! You might also want to invest in a screen that fits over the drain opening. This will help to keep your dog's excess hair from clogging your drains.

Unless your dog has a specific skin condition, such as dry, flaky, itchy skin, choose a mild shampoo designed specifically for dogs. Some shampoos contain harsh detergents that can dry the skin and damage the coat by stripping it of natural oils. Many shampoos and conditioning products are available, from all-purpose to medicating to herbal to color enhancing, so do not be shy about asking for help when choosing shampoos and conditioners.

Wet your dog thoroughly when giving him a bath.

How to Bathe Your Rottweiler

Saturate your Rottweiler with warm water (a cotton ball placed in each ear will keep the water out), apply a dab or two of shampoo, and scrub away! Work the shampoo into the coat with your fingers or a rubber massage tool designed specifically for dogs. Scrub from head to toe, being careful to avoid the eye area. To clean around a Rottweiler's eyes, wipe the area with a damp cloth. You can also use a small dab of tearless shampoo to gently wash around the head and eye area. Even though it is tearless, it is best to avoid getting any in your dog's eyes. Rinse his entire body thoroughly with warm water. The rinsing is the most important part.

A Rottweiler's coat can hold a lot of suds, and residual shampoo can irritate the skin, as well as leave a dull film on the coat. If necessary, shampoo and rinse again to be sure your Rottweiler is squeaky clean! If you are using a coat conditioner or skin remoisturizer, be sure to follow the directions carefully.

If possible, let your Rottweiler shake off any extra water, then towel dry him thoroughly. You can also use a shedding blade to help remove any excess water.

Throughout the entire bath, and until he is completely dry again, protect him from any drafts. If you live where the temperatures are warm and your Rottweiler is likely to air dry quickly, blow-drying is usually not necessary. If you choose to complete the process by blow-drying, hold the dryer at least 6 inches (15.2 cm) away from the coat, keep the dryer in motion, and use a low or cool setting to avoid damaging the coat or burning your Rottweiler's skin.

It is worth noting that damp dogs love to roll in whatever is handy, be it grass, dirt, mud, or gravel. You might consider keeping him sequestered in the house until he is dry. Otherwise, he can quickly undo all of your hard work!

Be careful not to brush the skin itself with a slicker or wire brush, because this can create nicks, scratches, and even welts.

BRUSHING

For most Rottweilers, a soft bristle brush, flat slicker brush, grooming glove, rubber curry brush, or shedding blade—a flexible saw-toothed device generally used for horses—is sufficient for whisking away pieces of debris, dust, dirt, and dead hair. Despite their seemingly carefree appearance, Rottweilers shed more than one might think. The amount of shedding, which is a natural process in which strands of hair die, fall out (shed), and are replaced by new hairs, varies according to the dog, the season, and climatic conditions. Most Rottweilers shed heavily in the spring and fall. Brushing helps to whisk away these dead hairs, promote and distribute natural oils, and bring out the shine and natural luster in a dog's coat.

How to Brush Your Rottweiler

Some breeders and groomers recommend starting at the dog's head—brushing the top of the head and around the ears, down the neck, chest, and front legs. Then brush in one long stroke from the head toward the tail, then down the sides, and finish with the rear legs. Others prefer starting at the feet and working upward.

Many groomers discourage backward brushing—brushing against the direction of hair growth—because it can damage the coat, and some dogs find the process uncomfortable and annoying. Either way, be sure to brush both the top coat and undercoat. Brushing only the top coat can result in painful mats and tangles that are difficult, if not impossible, to comb out. If a matted coat gets wet, the moisture is trapped near the skin, which can cause hot spots—circular lesions that are usually inflamed, raw, moist, and very painful. Remember, your Rottweiler's skin is sensitive, despite his brawn! Brush gently; don't tug or pull, because this can hurt. Be careful not to brush the skin itself with a slicker or wire brush, because this can create nicks, scratches, and even welts.

Regardless of which method you choose, once-a-week brushings are usually sufficient. However, a 5-minute, once-a-day once-over with a soft brush or glove is ideal to keep your Rottweiler's coat glossy and gorgeous and to keep shedding to a minimum.

Towel dry your Rottweiler thoroughly after his bath.

You can finish the coat and add shine by rubbing it down with a soft towel and spraying or rubbing on a coat oil.

As you brush, pay particular attention to the condition of his coat. A Rottweiler's coat is a mirror reflection of his health. Check to see:

- Is your Rottweiler's coat healthy and glossy? Or is it dull, brittle, and lackluster?
- Is his skin dry and flaky?
- Does his skin have a bad smell or that unmistakable doggie odor?
- Do you see bare spots where hair is missing?

Any of these conditions could be a sign of inadequate grooming, internal illness, parasite infestation, or an inadequate diet. When in doubt, a veterinarian can diagnose the problem and recommended suitable treatments.

Grooming Tidbit

After bathing your Rottweiler, be sure his collar and neck areas—especially the throat area—are thoroughly dry before putting his collar back on. A wet nylon or leather collar pressed against wet fur is an ideal site for bacteria growth. Equally important, if your Rottweiler swims in the family pool, ocean, ponds, rivers, streams, and the like, be sure to remove his collar until his neck and collar area (and his buckle collar) are completely dry. This will help to prevent bacteria and the unmistakable doggie odor that frequently accumulates in these areas. If your Rottweiler regularly swims in a chlorinated pool or in rivers, streams, and ponds—you may want to rinse him afterward to prevent skin irritations.

DENTAL CARE

Just as you take good care of your teeth, it is essential that you take good care of your Rottweiler's teeth. The importance of high-quality dental hygiene cannot be overstated. If left unattended, your Rottweiler can develop periodontal disease, a progressive disease that can, in advanced cases, lead to decayed gums, infection, and liver, kidney, and heart damage.

It is estimated that 80 percent of dogs over the age of 3 years have some stage of periodontal disease. And, like humans, dogs do experience painful toothaches, although some dogs may not physically exhibit signs of pain or the signs may be subtle and therefore overlooked by some owners.

Dental problems in dogs begin in the same way they do in humans—with plaque. Plaque is a colorless, transparent adhesive fluid, and it is the major culprit in periodontal disease. Plaque begins with the accumulation of food particles and bacteria along the gumline. Germs present in plaque attack the gums, bone, and ligaments that support the teeth, and routine home care can help remove this plaque. However, when left untreated, minerals and saliva combine with the plaque and harden into a substance called *tartar* or calculus. As the tartar accumulates, it starts irritating your dog's gums and causes an inflamed condition called *gingivitis,* which is easily identified by the yellowish-brown crust on the teeth and the reddening of gums next to the teeth.

In the early stages, *periodontal disease,* which results from the buildup of plaque and tartar around and under the gumline, generally is reversible, provided your Rottweiler receives veterinary attention along with sufficient and regular brushings at home. Otherwise, the process continues to erode the tissues and

85

bones that support the teeth, which can lead to pain and tooth loss. As bad as that sounds, it can get worse.

If the tartar is not removed, the cycle continues to repeat itself, encouraging even more bacterial growth. The tartar builds up under the gums and causes the gums to separate from the teeth; this causes even larger pockets in which more debris can collect. At this stage, your Rottweiler's teeth no doubt have quite an accumulation of highly visible, crusty, yellowish-brown tartar. Brushing your Rottweiler's teeth on a regular basis will remove plaque but not tartar. If your precious pooch already has a tartar build up, he will need to see a veterinarian to have it removed and his teeth polished.

In most advanced stages, damage from periodontal disease is considered irreversible because bacterial infection has been busy destroying your Rottweiler's gums, teeth, and bones. In addition, bacteria can also enter the bloodstream, causing secondary infections that can damage your dog's heart, liver, and kidneys.

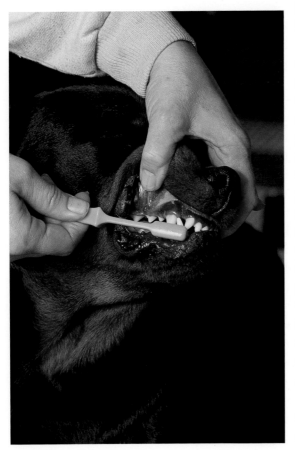

To brush your Rottweiler's teeth, lift the outer lips and expose the teeth.

In addition to home-care, a good dental hygiene program includes an annual veterinary exam. A veterinarian will check for potential problems, such as plaque and tartar build-up, gingivitis, periodontal disease, and fractured or abscessed teeth. If necessary, a veterinarian may recommend professional dental cleaning, also known as prophylaxis or prophy. While anesthetized, a dog's mouth is flushed with a solution to kill bacteria, the teeth are cleaned to remove any tartar, polished, inspected, and flushed again with an antibacterial solution, and fluoride is applied. Fractured teeth may require reconstructive surgery not unlike people receive, such as root canals and crowns.

The best way to prevent periodontal disease is to keep your Rottweiler's teeth clean. The process is relatively simple and

Chews and Food for Dental Hygiene

Chew Toys: You can try using any number of chew/dental toys available for dogs, like the ones made by Nylabone, that help to remove plaque. Select products that are right for the chewing style of your Rottweiler, and that are made to last. Toys should not replace brushing, but they will help to remove some of the plaque, exercise your Rottweiler's jaw, and satisfy his need to chew. Be sure to keep an eye on the toys and toss them when they get too small and become possible choking hazards. Be sure to avoid toys and bones that are hard enough to crack or break an aggressive chewer's teeth.

Food: Many veterinarians recommend avoiding table scraps and sweet treats, because they can increase the build-up of plaque. A high-quality, crunchy dog food may help to keep plaque from accumulating on teeth; however, this topic is highly debatable among the experts. Either way, a dry, crunchy food is most definitely better for exercising your dog's jaw. Veterinary dentist—approved dog food is available that is designed to help reduce plaque and tartar build-up. Your veterinarian can provide information on these products.

requires nothing more than a small number of fairly inexpensive supplies and a few minutes of your time.

How to Brush Your Rottweiler's Teeth

You will need a pet toothbrush, gauze for wrapping around a finger, or a finger toothbrush, which, as the name suggests, simply slides over your finger, and some toothpaste designed specifically for dogs. If you go with a pet toothbrush, be sure to get one specially designed for a Rottweiler or the mouth of a large-breed dog. A small toothbrush designed for, say, a Boston Terrier, will do little for your Rottweiler. A word of caution: Do not use human toothpaste. It is not designed for dogs and can upset your dog's stomach. Most canine toothpastes are formulated with poultry- or malt-flavored enhancers for easier acceptance.

As with other aspects of grooming, it is much easier to begin introducing oral hygiene to a puppy, but it is never too late to begin. You will need to start slowly and progress at a pace suitable for your Rottweiler. Most dogs, be they young or old, will no doubt take issue with a toothbrush being jammed in their mouth, so start by using your finger to gently massage his gums. Put a small dab of doggie toothpaste on your index finger and let your dog lick it. Praise him for being brave! Apply another dab on your finger, gently lift up his outer lips, and massage his gums.

Ideally, it is best to massage in a circular motion but, in the beginning, you may need to be satisfied with simply getting your finger in your dog's mouth. Try to massage both top and bottom,

Doggie Bad Breath

Also known as halitosis, bad breath is generally indicative of something more serious, such as periodontal disease, diabetes, kidney disease, or gastrointestinal problems. Unless you have seen your precious pooch eat something particularly offensive like spoiled garbage, squirrel guts, cat stools, or another dog's stools (or even his own stools)—yes, some dogs find this appetizing—it is best to have your dog examined by a veterinarian. If left untreated, some causes of bad breath can be indicative of severe and even fatal complications.

and the front gums, too. Watch out for those sharp baby teeth, and remember to keep a positive attitude, and praise and reassure your Rottweiler throughout the process. It is also helpful if you try to avoid wrestling with your dog or restraining him too tightly. This will only hamper the process and make him resistant to the necessary routine.

Depending on your dog, it may take a few days or a few weeks for him to accept you fiddling about in his mouth. Hopefully, he will eventually come to look forward to the routine. That is the long-term goal. It is possible he may never come to enjoy it, but it is important that he learns to accept it.

Once your dog is comfortable with this process, try using a toothbrush, finger toothbrush, or a gauze pad wrapped around your finger. Let your dog lick some toothpaste off the toothbrush or gauze pad and, again, praise him for being brave! This will help accustom him to the texture of the brush or gauze while building his confidence.

You are now ready to begin brushing. As before, lift the outer lips and expose the teeth. Most owners find it easiest to start with the canine teeth—the large ones in the front of the mouth. They are easiest to reach, and you should be able to brush them with little interference or objection from your dog. Once your dog is accustomed to you brushing a few teeth, progress to a few more, then a few more until you have brushed all 42 teeth (or 28 teeth if you have a puppy).

How Often to Brush

Ideally, you should strive to brush your Rottweiler's teeth on a daily basis, just as you do with your own teeth. Like anything else, the hardest part is getting started. However, once you accustom your Rottweiler to having his teeth brushed, you can incorporate it into your daily schedule. For instance, you might try incorporating it into your nightly routine, such as before you go to bed. You can make a production of it, so that your dog views it as a fun game you do together. Ask him in a happy, excited voice, "What are we going to do now?" Or, "Is it time to brush your teeth?" When you are done brushing, praise him for being brave. "What a clever boy!" If brushing every day seems an impossible task, try to brush your dog's teeth every other day or at least several times a week, because bacteria generally re-establish within about 20 minutes and tartar will harden within about 1 week. If your Rottweiler refuses to cooperate despite your best efforts—take him to your veterinarian for regular cleanings.

EARS

A Rottweiler's ear canal is warm, dark, and moist, and that makes it an ideal site for bacterial or yeast infections, tumors, and parasites, such as ear mites. Unlike a human's ear canal, which is a basically a horizontal line from the side of the head inward to the eardrum, a dog's ear canal is somewhat L-shaped. The internal ear canal descends vertically before making roughly a 45-degree bend and then a horizontal jaunt to the eardrum—also known as the tympanic membrane. Debris loves to collect in the 45-degree bend of the ear canal.

Ear Cleaning Supplies

- Ear-cleaning product for dogs
- Cotton or gauze pad

The key to preventing ear problems is to keep the ears clean, and to know the difference between a clean-smelling ear and a problem ear. A healthy ear should have a clean, healthy doggy smell—resembling the smell of beeswax, somewhat. A honey-colored wax in the ear is normal, but a crusty, dark substance may indicate problems, such as ear mites. An infected ear has an unmistakable foul odor. Ear infections are serious and should never be ignored or taken lightly. If your Rottweiler's ears have a discharge; smell bad; the canals look abnormal, red, or inflamed; or your dog is showing signs of discomfort, such as depression or irritability, scratching or rubbing his ears or head, shaking his head or tilting it to one side—these can be signs of a problem. You should seek veterinary attention right away. An ear infection left untreated can cause permanent damage to a dog's hearing.

To help prevent problems, you should get in the habit of examining your Rottweiler's ears regularly for wax, ear mites, and other irritations. If your Rottweiler walks or plays in pastures, fields, or areas with heavy underbrush—check them frequently for stickers, burrs, and other foreign matter.

How to Clean Your Rottweiler's Ears

To remove dirt and debris, use an ear-cleaning product specifically designed for dogs. Place a few drops of cleaner into the dog's ear canal and then gently massage the base of the ear for about 20 seconds. This helps to soften and loosen the debris. At this point, it is okay to let your dog have a good head shake to eject the cleaning solution and debris from the ear canal. Next, apply some ear-cleaning solution onto a clean cotton or gauze pad. Gently wipe the inside ear leather (ear flap), and the part of the ear canal that you can see.

Remember the old adage, "Never stick anything smaller than your elbow in your ear"? The same concept applies to dogs. Never stick cotton applicator swabs or pointed objects into the ear canal, because this tends to pack the debris rather than remove it. More important, you risk injuring your dog's eardrum should you probe too deeply.

If you suspect problems, seek veterinary attention right away and leave the probing to the experts.

To remove dirt and debris, use an ear-cleaning product specifically designed for dogs.

EYES

A Rottweiler's eyes should be clear and bright, and can easily be cleaned by saturating a gauze pad with warm water. Starting at the inside corner of the eye, gently wipe out toward the outside corner of the eye. If you notice excessive tearing, redness, swelling, discoloration, or discharge, these may be signs of an infection. If you suspect something is wrong, do not hesitate to call your veterinarian.

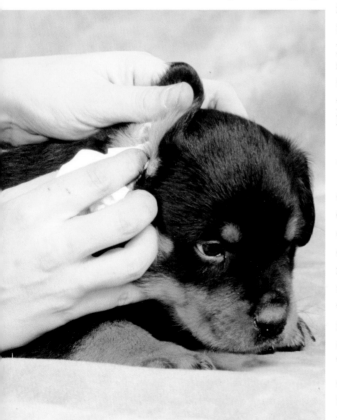

NAIL TRIMMING

Nail trimming is a necessary part of dog ownership. Few Rottweilers, especially those who spend the majority of their time indoors or on grass when outdoors, will wear down their nails naturally. If your dog's nails make an unmistakable click, click, click as he walks on hardwood, tile, or vinyl floors—his nails are too long. Ideally, a dog's nails should not touch the ground. This allows a dog to stand squarely and compactly on the pads of his feet. Nails that are too long put undue stress on the paw by forcing the weight onto the back of the pad. Equally important, nails that are too long can be broken, torn off, or snagged, and can scratch furniture, hardwood floors, and skin. Torn or broken nails can cause a Rottweiler a great deal of pain and discomfort, and they may become infected, which can require veterinary attention to remove the nail completely.

As with other aspects of grooming, it is best to introduce your Rottweiler to the practice of nail care at a young age, because some dogs can be a bit fussy about nail trimming. If you choose to clip the nails yourself, it is highly advisable to invest in a good-quality nail clipper designed specifically for dogs. In the beginning, depending on the puppy's level of cooperation, you may want to simply touch the nail clipper to the puppy's nail and then offer plenty of praise. Then progress to clipping tiny bits of nail and then trimming off the remaining dead nail in small bits.

In the beginning, you may need someone to help hold your dog, but once you get used to it, trimming your Rottweiler's nails is no more difficult than trimming your own. When in doubt, ask a veterinarian, groomer, or breeder to show you how to do it properly. Or have a professional trim them regularly, which can mean once a week or once a month—or somewhere in between—depending on the dog.

Nail Care Tip

As the nail grows, so too does the quick. For that reason, it is better to get in the habit of trimming tiny bits of nail on a regular basis, rather than waiting for the nails to get too long.

How to Cut Your Rottweiler's Nails

Owners are often reluctant to trim their dogs' nails for fear of hurting the dog or making him bleed. Dogs have a blood vessel that travels approximately three-quarters of the way through the nail, called the "quick." Clipping a dog's nails too short can cut the quick and cause bleeding. However, learning how to do it properly, using the correct equipment, and having a dog who accepts having his feet handled will go a long way in reducing the odds of inadvertently nipping the quick.

A Rottweiler's black nails can make it difficult to differentiate between the quick and the hook—the dead section of nail that extends beyond the quick. If you examine the underside of the nail before clipping, you will see that the section closest to the paw is solid, while the tip—or hook—of the nail looks hollow, like a shell. You may be able to see or feel the slightest groove on the underside, hook portion of the nail. Trim only the portion between the solid nail and the thinner hollow part—just tipping it where it curves slightly downward.

It is best to introduce your Rottweiler to the practice of nail care at a young age.

One of the easiest ways to trim the nails on the front feet is to have the dog sitting. Lift and hold one foot about 6 inches (15.2 cm) or so off the ground, so that you can see what you are doing, then trim away. With young or inexperienced dogs, you may have to put the foot back down between nails. Much will depend on how cooperative the dog is. With the rear nails, it is easier to have the dog standing: Lift the foot straight up off the ground about 4 or 6 inches (10.2 or 15.2 cm), and trim away. Some people find it easier to lift the rear foot and extend the leg backwards, not unlike the position a horse's leg is in when you are working on his feet. Some people have their dog lie on the floor—this works in a pinch, too. It is really a matter of preference, what is easiest, and what the dog will and will not tolerate.

If your Rottweiler has dewclaws, be sure not to overlook them in the trimming process. Dewclaws are the fifth digit on the inside of the front legs, usually an inch or so above the feet. If left unattended, they can curl around and grow into the soft tissue, not unlike an ingrown toenail on a human. Some breeders have the dewclaws removed, so your Rottweiler may or may not have them.

If You Cut the Quick

If accidentally nicked, the quick can bleed profusely and this bleeding can be difficult to stop. A number of blood-clotting products are available through retail stores, such as powdered alum, styptic powder, or styptic pencil. Having one of these products in your doggie first-aid kit is always a good idea. If you accidentally cut the quick, your Rottweiler will most certainly question your qualifications. He will no doubt be a bit tentative about continuing with the process. However, it is important that you resist babying or coddling him. It is difficult not to bundle him in your arms and kiss and fuss over him, but this will only feed into his fear and nervousness. Do not scold or manhandle him either. It is best to play with him for a few seconds to take his mind off the incident.

Nail Care Supplies

- Nail trimmer designed for dogs
- Styptic powder or pen in case of bleeding

Nail Files

Some owners prefer to file the dog's nails with an electric or battery-operated file. Some use a combination of both clippers and files. Electric or battery-operated files are not without hazards, however. They have an abrasive tip—similar to sandpaper—that spins at a high speed. If used incorrectly, an owner can apply too much pressure or file too close to the quick, causing a dog a good deal of discomfort. These types of instruments make whirling noises, and the vibration on the dog's nails can take some getting used to. If started at a young age, many Rottweilers will accept it as part of the routine grooming process. When in doubt, always seek advice from an experienced source when clipping or filing a dog's nails.

TRAINING AND BEHAVIOR
of Your Rottweiler

When it comes to training, understanding how dogs learn will greatly increase your chance of success and will help the process move along much quicker. Canine genetics and animal behavior are complicated and exhausting topics that go well beyond the scope of this book. The good news is you do not need a Ph.D. in genetics or animal behavior to figure out what makes your Rottweiler tick. Without delving too deeply into the complexities of canine genetics, it is safe to say that dogs do what they do for two reasons: 1) inherited behaviors, and 2) acquired behaviors.

Inherited behaviors—also known as genetic predispositions—are the traits that Mother Nature genetically preprogrammed. These traits are pretty much guaranteed to appear at some time in your dog's life whether you want them to or not. For instance, Rottweilers were bred to guard, and the instinct to guard is in their genes. If you put a guard dog in a fenced yard—he will guard. This inherent tendency to guard is part and parcel of your puppy's complete package. As a result, some Rottweilers can be arrogant, dominant, independent, and stubborn, and they do not like to be bullied.

By recognizing and understanding specific predispositions, you can learn to work within the confines of the breed—what the dog has and what he is built to do. You can learn to develop a particular style of handling that will get the best from your particular dog, and you can design a training program that best suits your puppy's individual and inherited characteristics.

Acquired characteristics are behaviors your puppy has acquired from the day he was born. These behaviors are learned—be they good or bad, desired or undesired. An 8-week-old Rottweiler, for example, who learns to have fun chasing young children and nipping their pant legs will see no harm in doing this as a 100-pound (45.4 kg) adult dog. An adorable puppy who is mollycoddled every time he whines or barks will grow into an adult Rottweiler who barks and whines whenever he wants attention. These are acquired behaviors—behaviors that a dog has acquired through learned experiences.

It is worth noting that acquired behaviors also can be positive. If, for instance, you call your 6-month-old Rottweiler, and he comes tearing over to you with his head and ears up, his tail wagging, and a happy attitude that screams, "Here I am!"—that too is an acquired behavior. The dog has learned to happily and eagerly come when called. Dogs who do not beg or steal food, bolt out doors, or run off have learned to respect their owners.

SOCIALIZATION

Before you even start thinking about training your Rottweiler, you must realize how important socialization is to forming a well-behaved pet. Certain periods in a puppy's life are critical in his social development. What happens within these individual stages has an enormous and significant impact on his future behavior as an adult. Research has shown that puppies are capable of learning at an early age, and they form lasting impressions during these critical periods. These impressions are remembered throughout a dog's life, be they good or bad.

Begin socializing your puppy as soon as possible.

A puppy who is exposed to positive experiences during the socialization period, such as handling, grooming, and different sights and sounds, stands a better chance of developing the socialization skills and coping mechanisms necessary to grow into a mentally sound and confident adult dog. Older puppies who have not been properly socialized during these periods tend to be more cautious. They generally grow up shy, fearful, and frequently nervous. As an adult dog, they find it difficult, if not impossible, to cope with new experiences. They rarely, if ever, reach their full potential or live their lives to the fullest. This is a disastrous situation for Rottweilers.

Socialization is the single most important process in a Rottweiler's life. Breeders and owners owe it to their puppies to take advantage of these critical periods to maximize their future, foster their zany personalities, and instill desired behaviors. How much time and energy you invest during this critical period directly impacts the future character of your puppy.

Early Socialization

By the time your puppy is ready to begin his new life at your home, usually between 7 and 8 weeks of age, the process of socialization will have already begun. The breeder will have seen your puppy through the neonatal and transitional periods and halfway through the critical socialization period. During this time, responsible and knowledgeable breeders will ensure that their litters are handled daily to accustom them to human contact and imprint trust, which is essential when it comes to raising a sound Rottweiler. They may have a radio or television playing to accustom them to different voices and sounds. They will make sure the puppies receive individual attention and are exposed to a variety of sights and smells in a safe and stress-free environment. Many breeders will have accustomed their young puppies to crates, thereby facilitating the crate-training process.

For this reason, you must make careful choices about where you acquire your Rottweiler. How your puppy is managed during the neonatal, transitional, and socialization periods has a tremendous impact on how he reacts and interacts to various situations and people as an adult dog.

Your Role in Socializing Your Rottweiler

Your job begins the day your puppy arrives at your home. There is much to accomplish and a very small window of opportunity, so it is important to maximize your time and use it wisely. Your Rottweiler must learn important socialization skills between 8 and 16 weeks of age. Once this small window of opportunity has passed, it can never be recaptured. If you dawdle or squander your opportunities during this critical time, your puppy will suffer in the long run. You run the risk of having your Rottweiler develop bad habits and associations that are difficult, if not impossible, to correct later in life.

As the owner of a new Rottweiler puppy, you are assuming the role of parent and leader. You are assuming an enormous responsibility that includes protecting him from bad or traumatic experiences while simultaneously instilling desired behaviors, fostering his personality, and providing him with every opportunity to grow into a well-adjusted, mentally confident adult dog.

The importance of maximizing your opportunities during this critical period cannot be overly stressed. Puppies mature faster than humans. On the average, humans take about 18 years to reach maturity, while puppies take about 1 to 1.5 years—depending on the dog. Your 8-week-old Rottweiler will be 8 weeks old for exactly 7 days. While 1 week may seem insignificant in the lifespan of a child, it represents a significant portion of your Rottweiler's puppyhood. Once those 7 days have passed, they can never be recaptured.

Therefore, if possible, avoid scheduling vacations or extended trips out of town while your puppy is between 8 and 16 weeks of age—unless, of course, you plan to take him with you. Boarding him in a kennel or leaving him in the care of friends or relatives during this time puts your puppy at a serious disadvantage later on in life. You will have missed a prime opportunity to foster his personality, shape his future character, and instill all the behaviors you want your puppy to possess as an adult dog.

How to Socialize Your Rottweiler

Before taking your puppy outdoors and around other animals, consult your veterinarian about any necessary puppy vaccinations to ensure that your Rottweiler is protected from diseases. Then, in a fun, safe, controlled, and stress-free environment, begin exposing your Rottweiler to a wide variety of people including children, teenagers, women carrying bags, men in floppy hats, other animals in the household, and so forth. You should expose your puppy to the clapping of hands, the jingling of keys, the clatter of dog bowls. He should explore a variety of surfaces including grass, cement, gravel, tile, carpet, linoleum, sand, and dirt. Many dogs—especially herding dogs—are attracted to moving objects, which incite their chase instinct. Your Rottweiler should be exposed to these objects, including strollers, wheelchairs, shopping carts, vacuums, bicycles, and kids on roller skates and skateboards. A puppy who is not exposed to moving objects may be fearful of them and may try to attack them as he gets older.

He should be exposed to stairways, wheelchair ramps, paper bags blowing in the wind, wind chimes, and horns honking. Let your puppy play in and around empty boxes, tunnels, or buckets. Allow him to investigate trees, rocks, bushes, branches, leaves, and fallen fruit. He should explore bugs and other animal odors, pastures, wooded areas, city sidewalks, and sandy beaches.

Enlarge your puppy's world and challenge his curiosity by taking him for rides in the car and walks in the park.

A well-socialized Rottweiler understands how to play nicely with other dogs.

Allow him to explore the many sights, sounds, and smells of a local dog show. Take him to the veterinarian's office or the local groomer for a cookie and a kiss. If you are interested in canine competition, expose him in a controlled atmosphere to the scents and sounds that he will encounter later in competition, such as agility or obedience equipment.

As your puppy's guardian of safety and well-being, you must protect your puppy from potentially harmful or fearful situations, yet not coddle or reward fearful behavior. Observe your puppy's reactions to different situations. Watch his ears and tail and body posture. Is he fearful? Apprehensive? Courageous? Dominant? Submissive? By understanding and reading your Rottweiler's body language, you will be able to evaluate and adjust the situation accordingly. For example, if your Rottweiler was raised in a childless environment, a room full of noisy, rambunctious children may be overwhelming or downright scary. By coddling or otherwise rewarding a puppy who shows fear, you reinforce that fear. Modify or restrict the exposure to one quiet, well-behaved child in the beginning until your puppy's confidence can handle more. When your puppy is brave, praise and reinforce him for being brave and inquisitive. "Good puppy!" or "Look at you. Aren't you brave!"

If you do nothing else for your puppy, you owe it him to make the time to properly and adequately socialize him during this critical life stage. This may seem time consuming, but it is a necessary investment when you choose to own a Rottweiler. His future well being depends on how much you do—or fail to do— during this critical period.

CRATE TRAINING

A crate is a fantastic training tool when used properly by responsible dog owners. Many owners look upon a crate as cruel or inhumane. Instead, it should be viewed from a dog's perspective. Before dogs became domesticated pets, they tended to seek safe, enclosed areas for security and protection. A crate mimics that safe, enclosed environment. Puppies, especially very young puppies, tire quickly and need a lot of sleep during the day. A crate, like the ones Nylabone makes, placed in a quiet corner of the kitchen or family room, encourages a dog's natural instinct to seek a safe and secure environment. When properly introduced, a crate becomes a safe-zone for your Rottweiler—a quiet place all his own to sleep, eat, and retreat from the poking, prodding fingers of noisy, rambunctious toddlers.

A key to successful puppy rearing is to never put your puppy in a position where he can get himself into trouble. Any puppy left unsupervised will develop bad habits. In record time, your adorable Rottweiler puppy can pee on the rugs, ransack the trash, and gnaw the leg off your dining room chair. Does the expression, "I just turned my back for a second!" sound familiar? During those short periods when you cannot watch your puppy closely, a crate prevents him from getting into mischief.

A crate is one of the safest, most successful, and efficient ways to housetrain a young puppy or adult dog. If your Rottweiler has an accident in his crate, the mess is much easier to clean and less damaging than when it is in the middle of your Persian rug.

A crate is also ideal for keeping your Rottweiler safe while traveling. A crated dog will not distract you from your driving responsibilities, teethe on your leather armrests, snatch the French fries from the cashier at the drive-up window, or eat your cell phone. Many motels and hotels, as well as friends and family, are more receptive to dogs provided they are crate trained. As your Rottweiler grows and matures, the crate will be his den and safe place for eating, sleeping, and retreating from the often chaotic and noisy world of humans.

Using the Crate

A crate, like any other training tool, has the potential to be abused. A crate is not intended for 24-hour confinement. Your Rottweiler should live with you and not in his crate. A crate should never be used as a form of punishment. It should provide your Rottweiler with a safe, secure environment. A place your Rottweiler enjoys.

Most puppies quickly learn to love their crates when it is associated with good things, such as feeding, treats, security, and sleep. To maximize the crate training process:

Crating Tip

Don't leave your dog confined to his crate for too long. He should see it as a pleasant and safe place to call his own, not as somewhere he is locked up and isolated.

- Make the crate attractive to your puppy by placing an old blanket, towel, or rug and a few of his favorite indestructible chew toys inside the crate. Remember, young puppies love to chew, so choose toys and blankets that are safe and do not present a potential choking hazard.
- Leave the crate door open and allow your puppy to explore in and around the crate. If your puppy goes inside the crate, praise him. "Good puppy!" or "Aren't you clever!" Reward him with a tasty tidbit while he is in the crate.
- If your puppy is reluctant to go inside, encourage him by letting him see you toss a tasty tidbit of food inside the crate, preferably toward the back of the crate. When your puppy goes inside the crate to retrieve the food, praise him. "Good puppy!"
- Feed your puppy his meals inside the crate, luring him inside with his food bowl. This makes the crate a positive place for your puppy to be.
- When your puppy is comfortable being inside the crate and shows no signs of stress, close the door for 1 minute. Do not latch the door. Open the door and praise your puppy for being brave! "Look at you! You're so brave!"
- As your puppy becomes more comfortable with the crate, gradually increase the time that he spends there. Never confine him for longer than 1 hour at a time—except at night when he is sleeping.
- If your puppy whines or cries, avoid reinforcing the behavior by letting him out of the crate or coddling him, such as saying, "What's the matter, honey?" Wait for him to be quiet for a minute or two before opening the door (provided you are certain he does not need to relieve himself).
- If you are working and cannot let your puppy out every hour, employ a reliable relative, friend, or neighbor to exercise your

puppy during the day. Or, try using a playpen or exercise pen. This will give your puppy room to play, exercise, and relieve himself if necessary.

HOUSETRAINING

The object of housetraining is to teach your puppy to relieve himself outdoors and not on your floors. As a general rule, Rottweilers are no more difficult to housetrain than any other breed. Some puppies can be more difficult to housetrain than others, but that has more to do with the individual puppy, rather than a reflection of the breed. The key to successful housetraining is vigilance and consistency on the part of the owner.

Housetraining is a relatively easy and painless process, yet it often causes owners a great deal of anxiety. Good planning and preparation and your unwavering commitment to the situation will provide your puppy with the best possible start. Crate training, when done properly, helps quickly and efficiently housetrain a puppy. If your puppy was born in the wild, he would live in a cave or den, and most den animals have an instinctive desire to keep their dens clean. As a result, they will try not to eliminate in their den. A crate serves as your puppy's den. If you watch a litter of puppies, you will notice that, around 3 weeks of age, the puppies will instinctively begin moving away from the whelping box to relieve themselves. This innate tendency to keep the den clean provide the foundation of housetraining using a crate. If you take advantage of this instinct, you reduce the chance of accidents. As your puppy matures, you gradually teach him to hold his bladder for longer periods of time.

To increase your chances of success while minimizing accidents, you must provide your puppy with a regular schedule of eating, sleeping, and eliminating. Dogs are creatures of habit, and they will have an easier time adjusting to their new household and a housetraining schedule if you provide some order and routine to their lives.

Understand Your Puppy for Housetraining Success

The first step in any successful housetraining program is recognizing that young puppies have very little or no bladder control until around 5 months of age. Puppies mature at different rates, so your puppy's control may develop earlier or later. A 7- or 8-week-old puppy is equivalent to a 4- or 6-month-old human baby. You would not expect a young baby to control his bladder, and it is unfair to ask your puppy to exercise control that he does not have.

Puppies are most active during the day—running, jumping, training, playing, exploring, and being a puppy. Because of their limited bladder size and lack of control, it goes without saying that they are going to need to relieve themselves many, many times throughout the day. During the night, however, puppies are usually exhausted from their busy day. They are more relaxed and, as a result, most puppies can sleep between 5 and 8 hours without having to potty. This varies from puppy to puppy, and in this sense they are not unlike human babies. Some parents get lucky and their babies sleep through the night. Others are relegated to months of sleeplessness.

If you have a puppy who wakes you up in the middle of the night or the early morning when he feels the need to go, it is best to get up with him rather than allow him to have an accident in his crate. While it may seem like forever, it will not be long before he can hold on all night.

For the first several months—until your puppy begins to develop some reliable bladder control—you will need to take him outdoors frequently. If you are 100 percent committed to a regular schedule, your puppy will learn that elimination opportunities occur on a schedule.

As a general guideline—to increase your chances of success

Your puppy will need constant supervision for successful housetraining.

Doing It on Cue

By going with your puppy, you also can begin instilling a verbal cue for the command, such as "Go pee" or "Go potty." A notable English trainer likes to use the cue "Go wee!" You can choose a separate word for urinating and defecating. Whatever cue words you choose, be sure they are words you are comfortable repeating in front of your kids, in-laws, and complete strangers. After all, you will be repeating them for 8 to 10 years, if not longer. These verbal cues should be given each time your puppy is in the process of urinating or defecating, otherwise you will teach him the wrong association. The words should be said in a calm but encouraging tone of voice. If your voice is too excitable, your puppy will most likely forget what he is doing and run to see what you are so excited about.

while minimizing accidents—take your puppy outdoors at the following times:

1. First thing in the morning when he wakes up.
2. About 15 minutes after drinking water.
3. About 30 minutes after eating.
4. Immediately after waking from a nap.
5. During any excitement, such as when you arrive home or guests come to visit.
6. At least once every hour during the day.
7. Last thing at night.

This guideline is for young puppies. Because puppies are individuals and must be treated as such, you may need to tweak or adjust this schedule to fit your puppy's individual needs. No one said raising a puppy was all fun and no work! Housetraining a puppy is a time-consuming endeavor, but time invested at this stage will make your life easier in the long run. It may seem unreasonable or unnecessary to take your puppy outside every hour to potty, but taking him out on a regular basis is easier, cheaper, and less aggravating than constantly cleaning or replacing carpets. Dogs are either housetrained or they aren't—the fewer mistakes your Rottweiler has as a puppy, the faster he will learn that outside is where he needs to go, and the more reliable he will be as an adult dog. It is worth noting that these steps work equally well when housetraining an adult dog—especially if you have acquired a rescue or shelter dog. In these instances, it is always best to assume he is not housetrained and begin the housetraining process from step one.

How to Housetrain Your Rottweiler

First thing each morning, when you hear that unmistakable whimper, let your puppy out of his crate and immediately take him outdoors to a designated spot. Do not dawdle or allow yourself to get sidetracked making coffee, checking your e-mail, or fumbling around for a leash—keep one in a convenient spot. A few seemingly insignificant minutes to you is long enough to guarantee an accident for your puppy. Remember, your puppy has been confined in his crate for several hours, and he just can't wait another minute. He needs to go right now!

While you are outside, watch your puppy to make sure he empties his bladder or bowels. It may take a few minutes, so be patient. When your puppy has finished doing his business, calmly praise: "Good puppy!" or "Good pee!" Once you have seen your puppy relieve himself outdoors, allow him supervised play indoors. If you take your puppy outdoors, and he does not relieve himself, it is important that you put him back in his crate for 5 or 10 minutes and then repeat the aforementioned steps. (If you are not using a crate to housetrain, you will need to keep your puppy where you can watch him for those 5 or 10 minutes.) Do this as many times as necessary until your puppy relieves himself. Do not assume your puppy has done his business. Seeing is believing, and you need to see your puppy empty his bladder or bowels. You will need to repeat this routine many, many times throughout the day and again just before you go to bed at night.

Never punish your Rottweiler for housetraining mistakes.

Why go to all this trouble? The importance of going with your puppy and watching him has many important purposes. First, if your puppy is on leash, take him to the same spot each time he needs to eliminate. This helps establish the habit of using a certain area of your yard. This also helps to keep your puppy on track and prevent him from getting too distracted with the potpourri of sights, smells, and sounds. Puppies are naturally curious and easily distracted. While sniffing the ground usually helps to speed up the process, if your puppy gets too distracted and forgets to go—when you bring him back indoors and he is no longer distracted, he will feel a sudden urge to go and it is highly likely that he will go on your carpet.

Young puppies, generally under the age of 3 months, find comfort and security in being close to you. If you leave while your puppy is searching for a spot to potty, he will most likely run after you and forget about the task at hand. If you put him outdoors and leave him to his own devices, it is highly likely he will

When Accidents Mean Something Else

Accidents are bound to happen during the housetraining process. But sometimes frequent accidents can signal a medical problem. You should seek veterinary assistance if you observe any of the following conditions:
• Change in color or odor of urine
• Change in frequency of urination
• Sudden change in the number of accidents
• Sweet or foul odor to the puppy

spend most of his time trying to get back in the house to be with you, and, again, he will have forgotten about the task at hand.

In addition, by going outside with your puppy, praise him for doing what you want—going to the bathroom outdoors. Praise will help your puppy to understand exactly what you want, and that will maximize the learning process.

Learning Signals

Where owners often run afoul is in thinking their puppy is housetrained when it is really only wishful thinking on their part. Puppies between the ages of 8 and 10 weeks do not show signs of having to urinate. When they have to go, they go right away—often stopping to urinate in the middle of a play session. It is unrealistic to expect your puppy to stop what he is doing and tell you when he needs to go outside. More often than not, your puppy will not realize he has to go until he is already going. Your job for the next 6 months, or longer depending on the puppy, is to keep an eye on your puppy and anticipate his bathroom needs.

Around 10 or 12 weeks of age, a puppy will start to exhibit signs—warning signals that he is about to urinate or defecate—by circling, making crying noises, sniffing the floor, or arching his back. Oftentimes, his tail will come up or he might stand by the door. This is where owners get over-confident and think they are home free. These are signs that your puppy is learning, not that he is housetrained. Now more than ever, you must remain diligent and stick to the program. Begin teaching him which signal to use to let you know he needs to go outside by reinforcing any or all of the signals.

By following these simple steps, your puppy will learn through repetition and consistency to relieve himself outdoors. Patience and consistency are the keys to housetraining. There are no short cuts. Do not backslide or slack off. You will only create problems that will exist for many years to come. The more often your puppy can do his business outdoors, the quicker he will learn, the happier you will be, and the sooner the entire family can get back to being barefoot in the house!

Accidents Will Happen

While it is in yours and your dog's best interest to keep indoor accidents to a minimum, few owners escape puppy rearing without

What To Do at Night

If your puppy wakes you up when he feels the need to go, and you find you simply cannot get up several times during the night—cover an area of the floor with sheets of newspaper. This works particularly well in a kitchen, which usually has a vinyl or linoleum floor. Set up an exercise pen on top of the newspaper and put his crate inside the exercise pen. At night, leave his crate door open. He will have access to his crate for sleeping, and he can also potty on the paper if he needs to go. The exercise pen will keep him confined to a small area.

This technique works in a pinch. However, it is worth noting that it is always worthwhile to make the effort to get up with your puppy if he needs to go outside, because teaching your puppy to urinate on newspaper can create its own set of problems.

an accident here or there. If an accident does happen, consider it your fault and be more observant in the future. Never scold or hit your puppy and never, ever rub his nose in the mess. Those are not housetraining techniques—they are crimes in progress. Punishing, yelling, or otherwise berating your puppy will only confuse him and prolong the housetraining process.

Scolding, punishing or berating your puppy is counterproductive to building a solid, trusting, and mutually respectful relationship. A puppy who lives in fear of you is likely to grow into an adult dog that is anxious and frequently worried. If he potty's on the floor, and you scold him when you get home 10 minutes or 2 hours later, it is highly likely that he will become anxious and perhaps fearful of being left alone, which can exacerbate urinating in the house or cause him to develop all sorts of unwanted behaviors as he grows into an adult dog.

TRAINING YOUR ROTTWEILER

Puppies and adult dogs learn through repetition and consistency. To provide your puppy with a basic foundation of obedience skills and manners that allow him to grow into a well-behaved adult dog and co-exist with humans, you must be consistent with your expectations. Dogs learn faster when the rules stay the same.

It is very important that your dog trusts you and does not feel he must worry about how you are going to react from day to day. For instance, it is unfair to allow an 8-week-old puppy to jump on you today, but scold him for doing so tomorrow when his feet are muddy. He does not have the mental ability to understand his feet are muddy and your white silk pants are expensive. If you do not want your adult Rottweiler jumping on you, you should discourage the behavior from day one when he is a young, impressionable puppy. It is unfair to allow your adorable puppy on the furniture today, but reprimand him for the same behavior when he is a 110-pound (49.9 kg) adult dog. Think ahead, and decide which behaviors you will or will not accept and which behaviors you can or cannot live with for the next 10 years.

Understanding the Individual

Equally important in the training process is understanding that all puppies are individuals. A litter of Rottweiler puppies may look alike, but they each have their own unique character, temperaments, and personalities and, as a result of their genetic make-up plus some environmental influences, they will grow into adult dogs who possess their own distinct qualities.

Using positive, reward-based training is a great way to bond with your Rottweiler.

If you have children, think how each was raised with the same amount of love, individual attention, rules, values, and so forth in order to make the most of their personalities and talents. Yet despite their seemingly uniform upbringing, each child is an individual with his own special talents, likes, dislikes, quirks, and idiosyncrasies.

Understanding your puppy's individual personality will help you to recognize which behaviors you can live with and those that might preclude a long and happy human–canine relationship. If, for instance, your puppy is bossy and pushy, begin right away discouraging the behavior of bolting out doors or grabbing food or toys from your hand without permission. If your puppy is a bit shy and nervous, expose him to safe situations that will help build his confidence, such as encouraging friends to get on the ground and talk to him, play with him, rub his tummy, and kiss his nose. Take him for rides in the car, to the veterinarian's for a cookie and a kiss, or trips to the neighbor's barn—on leash, of course—to see the horses and explore strange smells, sights, and sounds.

Types of Training

Many wonderful methods are available for training puppies and adult dogs. The hardest part is deciphering between the enormous variety of training methods and trainers. What works, what doesn't? Who's right, who's wrong? In today's canine-friendly environment, it seems that as many trainers and training methods exist as breeds of dogs. Positive and negative motivation, food training, play training, toy training, and clicker training—throw in the endless variety of paraphernalia employed, from electronic gizmos to metallic gadgetry—and the entire process can seem more complicated than computer science.

The good news is that Rottweilers are highly trainable and quick to learn, and raising and training a Rottweiler is not terribly difficult. It is well within the capabilities of most dog owners who set their mind to it. It does, however, require time, insight, dedication, and the ability to view setbacks with a sense of humor. Most Rottweilers love to work for and please their owners, but they do not like to be bullied. If you berate or treat them harshly, they are likely to tune you out and give up trying. They must be trained and handled with respect, fairness, and consistency.

A key ingredient to successful dog training is having a clear picture of what you want to accomplish and a well-thought-out game plan, which includes regular training, socialization, and interaction with your puppy both at home and in public. Additionally, it helps if you start right away—preferably as soon as your Rottweiler starts living with you.

Years ago, the accepted methodology of dog training was that a puppy had to be at least 6 months old before you began teaching basic obedience skills. That concept has since been debunked, and modern-day breeders, trainers, and animal behaviorists now recognize the important benefits of early training—as early as 8 weeks of age. Additionally, past trainers often employed the standard pop and jerk type training that involved a choke chain, force, and a total domination of the dog. While that method usually produced desired results, it often came at a hefty price that included stifling a dog's personality as well as his willingness and desire to please. Many of those methods produced dogs who obeyed commands out of fear rather than a desire to please their owners.

Today's top trainers had the foresight and willingness to change by recognizing the importance of allowing dogs and handlers to be themselves rather than imposing the same training method regardless of temperament. While trainers still exist who adhere to the ideology of force and domination as a means of training, most trainers employ gentler training methods that include praise, positive motivation, and positive reinforcement.

The concept behind positive motivation and reinforcement is that when a behavior has favorable consequences, the probability that the behavior will be repeated is increased. A dog learns to repeat a behavior, such as sit, down, or come, to receive a reward. The reward can be a combination of verbal or physical praise coupled with a tasty tidbit of food or his favorite toy.

Formal or Informal Training?

Owning a Rottweiler, or any dog for that matter, should be fun. Otherwise, what is the point? The same concept of fun should apply to training and playing. The goal is to teach your dog to cheerfully and eagerly respond to a variety of commands both on and off leash and under a range of circumstances, such as in your yard, at the park, and even when he is playing with his canine buddies. Where owners often run amok is in getting caught up in too much formal training and not enough fun, informal training. The primary difference between formal and informal training is the degree of precision. Formal training, however, does not mean all work and no play. It should be equally as much fun as informal training.

Successful training depends on understanding your dog.

Few owners are going to require their Rottweiler to respond with the precision of top-ranked obedience competitors. Nor are they necessarily interested in whether their dog sits perfectly straight, or if he took an extra step before he responded to the Down command. While these are matters of utmost concern to competitive trainers, most Rottweiler owners are quite happy when their dog sits on command or comes when he is called.

Puppy Kindergarten

If your Rottweiler is between 2 and 5 months of age, a puppy kindergarten class is an ideal environment for exposing and socializing him to everything he will encounter in his adult life. Puppy classes help your Rottweiler continue to expand

on his knowledge of canine communication and social skills that he learned from his canine mother and while interacting with his littermates. As he grows and matures, he will learn to communicate and interact with other dogs in a low-risk and stress-free environment.

Puppy classes should not be a free-for-all, where puppies play on their own while their owners socialize on the sidelines. A well-structured puppy class will include teaching basic obedience skills including fun puppy recall games, Sit, Down, and name recognition. You will learn how to read canine body language, how to train your puppy, and how to recognize problems early, before they become annoying, ingrained habits that are difficult to break.

Finding a Trainer

To find the right trainer or puppy class for you and your Rottweiler:

- Ask your veterinarian, breeder, dog groomer, or dog-owning friends for referrals. Word of mouth is a great tool for uncovering talented and knowledgeable trainers, while avoiding problem ones.
- Contact professional organizations that certify or recommend trainers, such as the Association of Pet Dog Trainers or National Association of Dog Obedience Instructors.
- Attend the classes of several trainers to observe their personalities, training techniques, and facilities.
- Look for trainers who focus on rewarding what your Rottweiler does right rather than punishing what he does wrong.
- Does the trainer recognize that dogs are individuals? Are the same training methods imposed on all the puppies, regardless of their mental maturity?
- Puppies learn best in low-risk, stress-free environments. Look for classes that are structured, run smoothly, yet still emphasize fun.
- Do the facilities provide a safe learning environment for you and your puppy? Are they well-lit, with matted floors and eight to ten puppies per class?
- Are the puppies separated—small puppies from large, young puppies from juniors, the rambunctious from the shy?
- Trust your instinct. Your puppy's safety and well-being are paramount. If you feel uncomfortable, find another trainer or puppy class.

Keep It Fun!

Regardless of whether you call it formal or informal training, maximize your dog's training by avoiding techniques that are repetitious, predictable, and boring for your dog. Rottweilers are intelligent, quick to learn, and always ready for a game. As a result, they also can become bored quite quickly, too. Therefore, use your imagination to be creative and come up with fun training techniques and games that stimulate your Rottweiler's mind and increase his desire to learn.

Start Small

Be sure to begin obedience training early in your dog's life, especially with a Rottweiler. He'll be a lot easier to work with before he reaches 100 pounds (45.5 kg)!

BASIC OBEDIENCE

The object of teaching basic obedience skills is to provide your Rottweiler with a set of commands he understands, thereby making your life and his more enjoyable. Trying to physically restrain a 100-pound Rottweiler who wants to zig when you want to zag is enough to make you wish you had bought a cat. A Rottweiler who does not have a solid foundation of canine manners and obedience skills can quickly grow into an unruly hooligan. A Rottweiler who is taught to respond reliably and quickly to basic commands is much easier and enjoyable to live with. No doubt, his life is more pleasurable because, as a well-behaved dog, he is more likely to be incorporated into the family environment rather than relegated to the isolation of the backyard.

Disciplining Your Rottweiler

No discussion on training or problem behaviors would be complete without a word or two about disciplining your Rottweiler. Only rarely should you need to discipline or correct a young puppy. The majority of your interactions should be positive and fun as you work toward building a solid human–canine relationship by instilling desired behaviors, discouraging undesired behaviors, and fostering his zany personality. Managing your Rottweiler so that he does not develop bad behaviors is critical.

It is much easier to create good habits through smart management and positive motivation than it is to go back and fix bad habits. You should take every opportunity to manipulate situations so that your dog does the right thing and can be rewarded. This is the essence of positive motivation and reinforcement. If left to their own devices, Rottweilers, like most puppies and adult dogs, will do what is in their best interest and that is seldom, if ever, conducive to living in a domesticated environment.

Before dogs were domesticated they lived in packs, where their survival depended on a hierarchal system. To coexist peacefully and guarantee their survival, the pack needed a clear chain of command. In a domesticated society, you must always be the top dog. Just as you set the rules and provide guidance and direction for your children, you must establish rules and provide guidance for your new puppy.

What Is a Correction?

During the adolescent stage, when your puppy begins to assert himself—perhaps challenging the chain of command—you may need to discipline him from time to time. Doing so correctly and effectively will ensure your Rottweiler puppy grows into a well-behaved adult dog that is a joy to live with, both at home and in public. Discipline should never be the staple of your puppy's training or the first line of defense when things begin to go wrong. Corrections should be reserved for completely unacceptable behaviors, such as when your puppy is biting you, your kids, or another dog. This type of behavior, if left unchecked, can be disastrous. Biting is unacceptable and should be stopped immediately, otherwise it is highly likely your Rottweiler will repeat the behavior as he grows and matures. Nothing spells disaster faster than a Rottweiler who thinks biting his owner is okay!

Also in adolescence, your Rottweiler may decide to deliberately ignore your command because he would rather sniff a bug, play with his canine buddies, chew on a bone, or any other myriad canine activities. An immediate correction will teach your Rottweiler that he must respond to you when given a command. That said, before correcting your Rottweiler, you must be absolutely certain your dog thoroughly understands and has heard the command.

It does not matter if your Rottweiler is 6 months or 3 years old, if you have not taught him the command, such as coming when called, it is unfair to correct him for not complying. You cannot correct your Rottweiler for something he has not learned. To do so is unfair and undermines the foundation on which a trusting human–canine relationship is built. When you correct a dog who does not understand a command or who is confused or worried, he will learn to fear rather than trust you.

Correcting or disciplining your Rottweiler does not mean he is bad. You are correcting the wrong choice and making the right choice happen. What constitutes discipline is different for every Rottweiler. The amount of discipline used will depend on your Rottweiler's temperament. For some Rottweilers, a change in your tone of voice coupled with an "Aaagh!" is enough. For bolder Rottweilers, a stern "NO!" may be in order.

Once you correct your dog, play with him for a few seconds to take his mind off the correction, and restore his happy attitude.

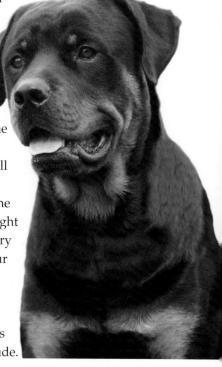

The Significance of Sit

The sit command is one of the most important ones your dog can learn, and it serves as the foundation for several other commands and tricks.

Once you have your dog's full attention, give the command again, and when he responds, reward him with plenty of praise.

TEACHING THE COMMANDS

The first step in teaching any exercise is to have a clear picture in your mind of what you want to teach. If you are teaching your Rottweiler to sit, have a clear picture in your mind of what a sit looks like. This may seem simple, if not downright silly, but if you cannot visualize it in your mind, how can you teach it and, more importantly, how can your dog learn it? Many owners have different ideas of what a sit or a down or even a come command represent. Some owners are happy if their dog comes on the eight or ninth command. Others want their Rottweiler to come the first time he is called. The choice is yours.

Dogs are naturally curious and love to explore and test their boundaries. Therefore, it is best to begin your dog's training in a familiar environment that has a limited amount of distractions, such as your house or yard. This is especially helpful if you are training a young puppy.

Puppies have limited attentions spans and are easily distracted by kids playing, toys lying around, birds flying overhead, a bug on the ground, cows mooing, horses whinnying, and so forth. It is unreasonable to expect a young puppy to ignore all the distractions and focus entirely on you.

Sit

Sit is a must-know command for every dog. A dog who understands the Sit command provides you with an avenue of control. Think of the many situations where your dog will need to know how to sit—at the vet's office, waiting to be fed, waiting to cross the street, or sitting and waiting while you open any door. The sit command increases his vocabulary and instills order in both your lives.

Teaching the sit command is relatively simple, and the guidelines are the same whether you are teaching a young puppy or an adult dog.

- Begin with your puppy on leash. This is especially helpful if your dog, like most puppies, has his own agenda, tends to wander off, or is easily distracted.
- Start with your leash in one hand, a tasty treat in the other

hand, and your puppy standing in front of you. (Hold the treat firmly between your thumb and index finger so that your dog cannot get it until he is in the correct position.)

- Show your puppy the treat by holding it close to and slightly above his nose. As your puppy raises his nose to take the food, slowly move the treat in a slightly upward and backward direction toward his tail, keeping the treat directly above his nose. (If your puppy jumps up or brings his front feet off the ground, the treat is too high. If he walks backwards, the treat is too far back or too low.)
- At this point, your puppy's hips should automatically sink toward the ground. As they do, give the Sit command. While your puppy is sitting, praise him with "Good sit!" and reward him with the tidbit. (Give the Sit command as your puppy's rear end hits the ground. Saying it too soon will teach the wrong association.)
- Release your puppy with a release word, such as Free or OK, play with him for a few seconds, and repeat the exercise three or four times in succession, three or four times a day.

Down can be one of the harder commands to teach.

Down

Down is an equally important and useful command. Use the Down command when you are watching television, sewing, preparing dinner, reading quietly, or when friends come to visit. Your dog may need to lie down on the vet's exam table, while you brush or scratch his tummy, check his coat for stickers and burrs, or when you want to massage his sore muscles.

Teaching the Down command can be a bit more challenging than the Sit, because it is considered a submissive position for some dogs. If your puppy has an independent personality, this exercise will take a bit more patience and persistence on your part. Do not give up! Remember, puppies learn through repetition and consistency.

Tips for Training Sit

- Get in the habit of saying the command one time. Avoid repeating yourself: "Sit, Sit, Sit, %#$@! SIT!" If you say it ten times, your Rottweiler will wait until the tenth command to respond.
- Make sure you give your puppy the release word before you allow him to rise out of the sit position. Doing so will clearly signal to the puppy the end of the exercise.
- Avoid saying Sit Down when you really mean Sit.

- Begin by kneeling on the floor so you are eye level with your puppy.
- With your puppy standing in front of you, hold a tasty tidbit of food in one hand.
- Let your puppy sniff the treat. Move the treat toward the floor between his front feet.
- When done correctly, your puppy will plant his front feet and fold his body into the Down position as he follows the treat to the ground.
- When his elbows and tummy are on the ground, give the command Down.
- While your puppy is in the Down position, reward with the treat and calmly praise: "Good down."
- Release your puppy with a release word, such as Free or OK, repeat the exercise three or four times in succession, three or four times a day.

Stay

The goal is to teach your dog to stay in a specific position, such as in a sit or down, until you say it is okay to move. It is useful in a variety of situations, such as when you want to answer or open the door without your Rottweiler bolting through it. To teach the Sit-Stay:

- Start with your puppy on a loose leash, sitting beside you.
- Tell your puppy to Sit and to Stay. Include a hand signal by holding the open palm of your hand in front of your puppy's face about 2 inches (5.1cm) from his nose as you say Stay.
- Watch your dog closely for the slightest movement that may indicate he is about to stand up or lie down. Be proactive in your training by reminding your dog to stay before he moves.
- Once he has remained in position for a few seconds, praise calmly and warmly with "Good stay" and a treat. Include calm, physical praise, such as gentle stroking—but not so enthusiastically that he gets excited and forgets the task at hand.
- As soon as you see any movement, repeat your Stay command firmly, but not harshly.
- If your dog stands up, use your leash to prevent him from moving away and get him into the sit position again. If he lies down, gently reposition him and remind him to stay.
- Reward him with a treat first and then release him with an OK or Free command. (If you release your dog first and then

reward him, you will teach him the wrong association. He will think he is being rewarded for moving. This can teach a puppy to anticipate the reward, thereby encouraging him to break the Stay command.)

- As your puppy matures and can remain sitting beside you for 2 or 3 minutes without moving, progress by giving the Stay command and then stepping directly in front of his nose. Gradually begin increasing the distance between you and your puppy.
- Once you have a reliable Sit-Stay in a nondistractive situation, begin incorporating mild distractions, such as toys lying nearby on the floor. As your dog becomes reliable with mild distractions, begin escalating the distractions. Try training while other people or dogs play nearby. If your dog has a difficult time focusing on the task at hand, perhaps the increase in distractions was too soon or severe.

To teach the Down-Stay, begin with your dog in the Down position, and tell him to Stay. Then follow the remaining instructions for the Sit-Stay.

Come

The goal is to teach your puppy to come to you reliably, willingly, and immediately—without hesitation—upon hearing the Come command, while in a wide range of situations, such as at the park, in the neighbor's yard, at a friend's house, in an emergency, or any time he gets loose. It should never mean in your dog's mind, "OK I hear you. I'll be there as soon as I finish chasing this bug." You want your dog to understand that when you say "Come!" it means, "Stop what you are doing and run back to me as fast as you can—right now." In the beginning, you teach this behavior with fun games and tasty rewards. Ideally, as he grows into an adult dog, you want him to come to you because he wants to be with you—not just because you have a cookie. This is why it is so important to connect with him mentally—to establish a strong human–canine bond.

Don't use the Come command for anything your Rottweiler might dislike, or to end playtime. When you call your puppy, you should do something silly with him when he gets to you, such as a quick game of tug, a fun trick, or reward him with a tasty tidbit, and then let him run off and play again. Owners often make the mistake of calling their puppy only when it is time to go in his

Tips for Training Down

- Make sure you give your puppy a release word before you allow him to rise out of the down position. Doing so will clearly signal the end of the exercise.
- Get in the habit of saying the command one time. Avoid repeating yourself: "Down, Down, Down, I said DOWN!" If you say it ten times, your Rottweiler will wait until the tenth command to respond.
- Be careful not to use the command Sit Down when you really mean Down.
- Avoid confusing your dog by using the Down command when you really mean off—such as getting off the furniture or not jumping on you.

Tips for Training Stay

- Many puppies are not emotionally mature enough to cope with this exercise until they are 5 or 6 months old. If this is the case with your puppy, do not force the issue. Simply wait until he is older and mentally more mature to understand and cope with the exercise.
- When first learning this command, 5 or 10 seconds in the Stay position is long enough for most dogs.
- Gradually, over a number of sessions and in 5-second increments, increase the time your Rottweiler remains in position.
- Do not be in a hurry to move away from your dog or have him hold the position for longer periods.
- Young puppies have limited attention spans. How fast your Rottweiler progresses with this exercise will depend on his mental maturity.
- Do not nag, scold, or send him threatening looks during a Stay. Dogs who are bullied or intimidated into staying are less reliable in the long run. Dogs learn faster and retain more information when they learn in a stress-free environment.
- Never leave your dog in a Stay position unsupervised, such as outside a store or anywhere he could run off, be hurt, stolen, or lost.
- Avoid using the Stay command when you really mean Wait, such as wait in the yard, or wait in the car until I get back.

kennel or to put his leash on and go home. In these situations, your puppy will quickly learn that Come means the end of his freedom, and he is likely to avoid you the next time he is called.

When teaching the Come command, call your puppy only when you are absolutely certain he will respond. For example, if you call your puppy when he is excited about greeting another dog, when a family member has just come to visit, or when he is eating his dinner—he will be too excited and distracted to respond to your command, and you will inadvertently be teaching him to ignore you. In the early stages, when your puppy is learning the Come command, it is prudent to wait until the excitement has subsided and then call him to you. If you must have your puppy come to you during these times, it is better to go and get him rather than call him to you.

Equally important, take advantage of opportunities where you can set him up to succeed by calling him back to you when he would be coming to you anyway, such as when you have just arrived home and he is running toward you, or when you have his dinner or a tasty tidbit. Let him know how clever he is when he gets to you.

A puppy who views Come as a fun game is more likely to develop a reliable response to the command. If this behavior continues throughout his puppyhood, and you remain excited and enthusiastic each and every time he comes to you, he will have a strong and positive response to the behavior as he grows and matures into an adult dog.

Use an informal game like Find me! to begin teaching Come in a positive, fun, and exciting manner. This game capitalizes on a dog's natural chase instinct. It is also an excellent game for instilling the Come command in young puppies.

- Start with a pocket full of tasty tidbits.
- Rev your puppy up by showing him a yummy treat and then toss the treat down the hallway or across the living room.
- As your puppy runs for the treat, you run in the opposite direction and hide behind a chair or door as you say his name enthusiastically.
- When your puppy finds you, make a big fuss: Get on the floor, roll around, and lavish him with a potpourri of kisses and praise. "Good come!" or "You found me!"
- Repeat the game several times throughout the day, but not so many times that your dog becomes bored.
- You can also play this game outdoors. Be sure to play in a fenced area to protect your dog from harm or prevent him from running off. When you are outside in your garden or yard with your dog, and he stops to sniff the grass or explore a bug—duck behind a tree or bush, clap your hands, and say his name in an exciting tone of voice.
- When your dog gets to you, greet him with plenty of hugs, kisses, and praise, "Good come!" or "Good boy!" It is not necessary for your dog to sit before he gets a treat. If you insist on your puppy sitting first, you will not be rewarding the most important part of the exercise, which is coming to you.

Leash Training

Walking a 100-pound (45.4 kg) Rottweiler who wants to zig when you want to zag is a frustrating challenge for even the most patient (and strongest!) owners. There are several variations to walking on leash. The formal Heel command is used by most obedience competitors who are sticklers for precision.

Reward your dog with a treat after he performs the sit.

They spend years teaching their dogs to walk with their head and body in a specific position. Most Rottweiler owners are not going to require that much precision. They are quite happy if their dog is not dragging them down the street.

While the traditional heel position is on the handler's left side, there may be times when you do not care if he is on your left side, right side, or walking out in front of you. That said, it is always easier to teach your puppy to walk on leash by starting on the left side and sticking with it until he understands the exercise. Once he has mastered walking nicely on leash, allow him to walk on the right side or out in front of you.

Getting Started with Very Young Puppies

Begin leash training in a familiar, quiet, and nondistractive environment.

It is important that your puppy not associate his leash and collar with a barrage of corrections or nagging. He should view walking beside you as something fun you do together.

To begin:

- Always teach this exercise on a buckle collar, never a choke-chain.
- Attach a leash (or thin long-line) to his collar and allow him to drag it around. Don't worry if he picks it up and tries to carry it around. In fact, put a command to the behavior. "Have you got your leash?" eventually becomes "Get your leash!"
- When your puppy is happily dragging the leash, pick it up and start walking forward, encouraging your puppy to walk close to your left side by talking sweetly to him and luring him with a tasty tidbit from your left hand. (This is easier if the leash is in your right hand.)
- When you have walked a few steps with your dog on your left side, reward him with the tidbit of food. Remember to verbally praise and offer the food reward when he is close beside your left leg. This will encourage him to remain in position.
- Once your puppy is comfortable walking beside you, begin teaching a more formal "walk nicely on leash."

Training Tidbits for Puppies

- Only reward sensible walking. If your puppy is jumping and lunging for the food, hold the food lower and in front of his nose, but do not give it to him until he takes two or three steps without jumping.
- If your puppy is not interested in following you—slow down and be more obvious with the lure. You may need to get a tastier lure or reward more frequently.
- If your puppy freezes on the spot and won't move—do not drag him around or force the issue. Try this: Drop the leash and run away while clapping your hands. Very young puppies like to follow their owners. Most likely, he will see you running away and try to catch you. When he does, praise him for finding you. "Good boy!" Nonchalantly pick up the leash, start walking, and encourage him to walk close to your left side by luring him with a cookie and talking sweetly to him. Take two or three steps, praise, and reward.

Walk Nicely on Leash

The goal is to teach your puppy to walk nicely on leash—anywhere within the full extension of his leash, on either side of you, or in front of you—without pulling. He also should learn that a loose leash means he goes forward. Highly rewarding! Pulling on the leash means he stops. Definitely nonrewarding! Puppies who learn not to yank their owner's shoulder out of the socket grow into adult dogs that do not pull on their leash. They are a joy to own because it is fun to take them for walks, and they are more likely to be included in family outings.

To begin:

- Teach this exercise on a buckle collar, never on a choke-chain.
- With your puppy on leash, encourage him to stand close to your left leg by luring him into position with a tasty tidbit of food.
- Praise and reward him with the tidbit when he gets there. "That's my boy!" (Teach a separate command for getting into position on your left side, such as "Close" or "With me." When he is in the position you want, for example, on your left side, reward him with the tidbit and praise, "That's your Close" or "Good Close!"

Tips for Teaching Come

- Your dog must always chase you. Avoid making a game of you chasing your dog, and never allow kids to chase your dog. It inadvertently teaches him to run away from you, which creates many problems down the road.
- If you want a dog who reliably comes to you when called, the Come command must always be positive.
- If your puppy comes to you, you must always, always, always praise him — even if moments before he chewed your shoes, urinated on the floor, or ransacked the trash. There are no exceptions to this rule.
- Never call "Come" and then correct him for something he did, such as chewing your shoe or urinating on the floor. Punishing him when he gets to you will only make it less likely that he will come back the next time. If you want to correct your dog, go and get him. Do not call him to you.
- Do not call "Come" if you want to give him a bath, administer medications, or anything else he might find unpleasant. Instead, go and get your dog and then put him in the tub, trim his nails, administer medications, etc.
- Never allow your puppy to run off leash in an unfenced or unconfined area. Doing so puts your puppy at risk and teaches him bad habits, because he is too young to reliably respond to the Come command.
- Once your puppy develops a reliable response to the Come command — meaning he comes each and every time he is called — begin teaching this exercise in more distracting circumstances.

Eventually the dog will learn to associate "Close"—or whatever command you choose—with being in position on your left side.)

- Show him the tidbit of food. When you have his attention, hold the food ever so slightly above his nose, just high enough so that his head is up and he can nibble the food without jumping up. With the food in his face, say his name and give your command for walking on a loose leash (i.e., "Fido, let's go") and then start walking forward.
- Keep your right hand (the one holding the leash) close to your body. This will keep the leash length consistent. As you walk forward, watch the leash. If it begins to tighten, stop walking and stand still. Most likely, your puppy will come to an abrupt halt and look back at you as if to say, "What the heck!"
- Stand still and encourage your puppy back into position with the tidbit of food. Avoid moving or turning in circles to reposition your puppy. A dog cannot find your left side (i.e., heel position), if your left side is constantly moving.
- When your puppy is repositioned on your left side, repeat these steps until he is walking beside you without pulling on the leash. When you have taken a few steps, stop, praise, and reward him while he is beside you. If you reward him when he is not in the correct position, you will have inadvertently taught him the wrong association.

- When your puppy is walking beside you, tell him he is smart and clever. Chat sweetly to him to encourage him to walk beside you. Over time, gradually increase the number of steps he is walking on a loose leash, but don't go so far that he gets out of position and begins pulling on the leash. The goal is to gradually increase the length of time between "Let's go" and rewarding with the treat.
- In the beginning, treats are used to lure the dog into the correct position and show him what you want him to do. Once he understands walking nicely on leash, begin keeping the treats in your pocket and rewarding him less often.

PROBLEM BEHAVIORS

In a perfect world, puppies and adult dogs would never get into trouble! In the real world, however, it is unrealistic to expect any dog to go through his entire life without getting into some sort of mischief or developing an annoying habit or two. It is important to remember that dogs, like kids, are first and foremost individuals. No two are alike, and they must be treated as individuals to maximize their potential. Their temperaments can fall within a broad range of characteristics, and they can develop their own quirks and idiosyncrasies.

That said, annoying or offensive behaviors do not suddenly appear—they are learned. Dogs do not do anything you do not allow to happen. Puppies and adult dogs do not pee from one end of the house to the other just to annoy you. Their brains are not hardwired to be vindictive. If your dog is urinating in the house, it is because he is not housetrained, and he is not being supervised.

Equally important, puppies do not magically outgrow problems. A puppy that digs holes in your garden will not suddenly stop digging, regardless of how much you hope and pray. If you do not want him digging up your favorite rose bushes, you need to modify his environment so that he is not put in a position where he is allowed to get himself into trouble.

Barking (Excessive)

Overall, the Rottweiler is by no means a noisy dog. However, it is natural for dogs to bark or otherwise vocalize. They bark for a variety of reasons. They bark when they get excited, when they are playing with other dogs, when the doorbell rings, and to greet you when you arrive home. If you have done enough proper socialization, your Rottweiler will not regard every little noise or visitor as a threat.

Your Rottweiler's barking will no doubt be reasonable and appropriate, such as to alert you to suspicious intruders or unexpected visitors. Most well-socialized adult Rottweilers have an innate ability to protect their territory and will alert-bark without being taught to do so. If your Rottweiler can be quieted with a single command, you probably do not have much to worry about. Problems arise when your dog is too hyped to stop barking. Therefore, it is best to curtail any problems immediately. This includes never encouraging your Rottweiler to bark. For instance, when the doorbell rings, avoid asking your Rottweiler, "Who's there?" or "Let's go see!" This can excite your Rottweiler and encourage him to bark. It may seem like a fun game when he is 10 or 12 weeks old, but it is a difficult and annoying behavior to stop once it becomes ingrained.

If your puppy is barking as an attention-seeking behavior, ignore him until he quiets. Then calmly praise, "Good Quiet!" or "Good Boy!" Whatever you do, do not verbally or physically acknowledge your dog's barking. By shouting "NO!" or "Quiet!" the dog is likely to think you are joining in. "This is fun! Mom is helping me make a lot of noise!" This only encourages the unwanted behavior.

Teach the Come command in an enclosed area where your dog cannot run off.

Equally important, in a dog's mind, negative attention is better than no attention at all. By verbally responding to your dog, you

Tips for Walking on a Leash

- Always begin training in a familiar, quiet, and nondistractive environment. Your backyard, living room, or family room is ideal.
- Use random rewards and tasty tidbits (i.e., boiled chicken, leftover steak, turkey wieners) to keep your puppy interested and motivated.
- When first teaching this exercise, be sure to have a tidbit of food in your hand before starting. If you fumble in your pocket for food after your puppy has done an excellent job, he will be out of position and you will have lost the opportunity to reinforce the correct position. Remember, timing is everything when training dogs!
- Always dispense the food from your left hand. This keeps your puppy from crossing over in front of you—tripping you in the process—to get the tasty tidbit in your right hand.
- If you do your part when your puppy is younger and still receptive to learning, then pulling and tugging on the leash is not a problem as he grows bigger and stronger.
- Teaching a puppy (or adult dog) to walk on leash takes time. Be patient. You will need to repeat these steps over and over before your dog gets the hang of it.

are inadvertently giving the dog what he wants, which is attention. As long as everyone in the family ignores the attention-seeking barking, your dog is likely to lose interest and quickly give it up as a fruitless venture that does not offer any reward.

It is best not to soothe or otherwise coddle your Rottweiler when he is barking. This too will inadvertently encourage the unwanted behavior. If your dog is barking and you are telling him, "It's okay, honey. Mommy loves you," the dog thinks he is being rewarded for barking. In the dog's mind, he is thinking, "When I bark, my mom tells me it's okay. So I should keep barking."

Most barking problems can be avoided if you plan ahead and have a clear picture of the behaviors you will and will not accept. However, if your Rottweiler has already developed a barking problem and is well on his way to wearing out his welcome, try a shaker can as a training aid coupled with positive reinforcement.

Using a Shaker Can

Shaker cans make a lot of noise and that's what you want! The concept is that the noise from the shaker can interrupts your dog's barking and, once the dog's barking behavior is interrupted, praise and reward him for not barking.

Shaker cans are easy to make—simply fill an empty soda can with a dozen or so coins or small pebbles and tape the opening closed. As soon as your Rottweiler begins to bark—for instance, when the doorbell rings—immediately give a command, such as Quiet,

Enough, or No Bark, and shake the can. If done correctly, the noise should be loud enough to startle the dog and interrupt his barking. When he stops barking, immediately praise: "Good Quiet!" or "Good Boy!" Reinforce the behavior with a tidbit of food, but be sure to do so when the dog is not barking. Otherwise, you will be teaching the wrong association and inadvertently reinforcing the barking.

Keep multiple shaker cans strategically placed around the house—near the telephone, front door, bedroom, living room—for convenience and accessibility. If you house your dog outside, have shaker cans strategically located outdoors, as well.

A word of caution: Place the shaker cans out of your Rottweiler's reach. Aluminum cans are sharp and dangerous when punctured or torn. Rottweilers, curious creatures that they are, can cause serious damage to their teeth, tongues, mouths, and stomachs if they chew on the can. Once a Rottweiler gets the can open, he may try to swallow the coins, which presents a potential choking hazard. Most important, never throw the can—or any other objects—at your Rottweiler. You may injure or frighten him, and he will most likely learn to fear you.

Managing Your Rottweiler

The best prevention against future barking problems is smart dog management.

Socialization with other dogs can help prevent future problems.

- Never allow your puppy or adult Rottweiler to be put in a situation in which he is allowed to develop bad habits, such as leaving him in the backyard unsupervised all day where he is inspired to bark at constant stimuli including other dogs

Seven Tips for Successful Dog Training

- Puppies and young dogs have limited attention spans. Keep sessions short: train two or three times a day, five or ten minutes per session.
- Training must always be fun. Fun games maximize your dog's propensity to learn.
- Train when your dog is awake and eager to play. Never wake your dog to train him.
- Dogs learn at different rates. Train within your dog's mental and physical capabilities. Never progress at a speed faster than your dog's ability to comprehend.
- Set achievable goals to keep you and your puppy motivated. Keep training steps small, and praise your dog every time he does a tiny step right.
- Always use a command when you use your dog's name. "Fido, come!" or "Fido, down." If you repeatedly say your dog's name without putting a command with it, it is a form of nagging and eventually your dog will become desensitized to his name.
- Always end a play/training session on a positive note.

barking, a cat on a fence, a bird overhead, leaves falling, neighbors coming and going, and life in general.

- Barking at environmental stimulation is often self-rewarding for the dog. A dog barks at the postman and when the postman leaves the dog thinks, "Look how clever I am! My barking made that man leave!"
- A Rottweiler housed indoors also can develop barking habits. If he sits on the furniture and stares out the living room window, he may be encouraged to bark at stimuli, such as neighbors, other dogs going for a walk, kids on bicycles, or the UPS man.
- If your dog barks while in the excitement of play—stop the game immediately. When your dog stops barking, praise: "Good Quiet!" or "Good Boy!" Once you have regained control of the situation, begin playing again.

Chewing

It is hard to imagine an adorable 10-week-old Rottweiler puppy as a one-dog demolition team. However, do not let their cute looks deceive you. Rottweiler puppies, like most puppies, can be incredibly aggressive chewers and wreak havoc in your household. They can destroy drywall, carpet, drapes, and linoleum. They can turn your favorite pillows into confetti, shred your bedspread, destroy electrical cords and potted plants. They will gladly shred magazines, books, and anything else they can get their teeth on—and that's in the 15 minutes it takes you to drive to the post office and back!

If you must leave—even for 2 minutes—take your Rottweiler with you or confine him in a crate, exercise pen, or kennel. Do not

Teach Your Rottweiler Right from Wrong

Until your puppy is reliable, it is wise not to give him free run of the house. Remember, puppies are individuals. It is impossible to arbitrarily put an age on when a puppy is reliably trained. Some puppies have a stronger desire to chew than others. A general guideline is about 1 year of age. However, much of this also depends on how conscientious and committed you are to managing your puppy's environment, instilling good behaviors, and discouraging unwanted behaviors.

As your puppy grows and matures, his desire to chew will diminish. It is important, however, to continue giving him bones and chew toys throughout his life to exercise his jaws, keep his teeth clean, and entertain him for a few hours.

If you allow your Rottweiler puppy supervised excursions into the rest of the house, you will be able to monitor his whereabouts and, in the process, provide him with appropriate chew toys. If, for instance, you are watching television, have one or two chew toys available for your puppy. You may need to encourage him by showing him the toy. When you see him settle down to chew on it, calmly praise him. Then allow him to chew without interruption. Tether him to the leg of the couch or coffee table with a lightweight leash to prevent him from wandering off.

put your Rottweiler in a position where he can develop bad habits. This point cannot be emphasized enough. Puppies chew, especially when they are teething. If you leave your Rottweiler unattended or unconfined while you run to the mailbox or take a quick shower, you should not be surprised when you find the heel missing off your favorite pair of leather shoes.

Prevention Is Key

Few owners escape canine ownership without losing a slipper, a pair of rubber goloshes, or a potted plant. Puppies are going to chew. It is a fact of life. However, the key to minimizing destruction and preventing bad habits is management. Never allow your puppy to be put in a position where he can get himself into trouble or develop bad habits. Any puppy left unsupervised is trouble looking for someplace to happen.

If you allow your puppy free run of the house, you should not be surprised when you come home to find epic amounts of destruction. It is equally unfair to scold or otherwise punish a puppy for your temporary lapse of good judgment. Therefore, to foster good habits and minimize destructive behaviors, follow these simple guidelines:

- Before bringing your new puppy home, plan ahead. You should have an exercise pen or play pen and a crate ready. Do not wait until you need them. If you have a Rottweiler, you will need them.
- When you cannot keep a constant watch on your puppy, keep him confined in an exercise pen, play pen, crate, or puppy-

proofed area with his favorite chew toy. This includes when you need to jump in the shower for 5 minutes, while you are making dinner, or when you dash outside for 2 seconds to move the sprinkler.

- Once your puppy arrives at your home, know where he is and what he is doing at all times. You would never dream of taking your eyes off a toddler, and you should not take your eyes off a Rottweiler puppy when he is not safely confined.

- Puppy-proof your home. Puppies are ingenious when it comes to finding items to chew on. Pick up anything and everything your puppy is likely to put in his mouth including shoes, purses, jackets, schoolbooks, candles, rugs, electrical cords, dolls, and so forth.

- Make sure your Rottweiler receives plenty of exercise each day. Puppies and adult dogs require daily physical and mental stimulation. Lacking appropriate and adequate exercise, they will release pent up energy through chewing, digging, or barking.

The Importance of Chew Toys

A variety of chew toys are available in all sizes and shapes to entertain your Rottweiler for an hour or two. Chew toys satisfy your puppy's need to gnaw on something while diverting him from chewing on inappropriate items. While some chew toys are better than others, no scientific formula exists for finding the right chew toy. Most times, it is a matter of trial and error. Avoid toys or bones that are too hard and may crack your dog's teeth, or ones that are too small or break apart and present choking hazards.

- Chews are available in a wide variety of shapes, sizes, and products, including beef muscle, pig ears, smoked hog hide, dehydrated pig snouts, and tightly rolled rawhide. Some colored rawhide chews can stain carpets and furnishings. Cow hooves, while a popular canine favorite, are hard and can chip or break your dog's teeth.

- Specially designed rigid nylon and rubber bones and toys are excellent for satisfying your puppy's need to chew.

- Rope toys and tugs often are made of 100-

Eyes on Size

Make sure your Rottweiler's chew toys are appropriate to his size and chewing power. Toys that would be just right for a smaller dog can pose a choking hazard to a full-grown Rottie.

percent cotton. They are frequently flavored to make them more attractive to your puppy or adult dog. Some have plaque-fighting fluoride floss woven into the rope to deep-clean your dog's teeth and gums. Be careful your puppy cannot shred the cotton ropes, which may be a potential choking hazard.

- Plush toys vary in their durability. Some are easily shredded by the tenacious, seek-and-destroy Rottweiler who can chew out the squeaky part in record time, while other dogs like to carry them around or snuggle with them. When choosing these toys, opt for the durable models if your puppy is likely to shred, disembowel, and then attempt to consume the innards.

- A super-size carrot is often a good chew toy for young puppies. They are tasty, durable, easily digestible, and puppies love them. Stay away from raisins and grapes, which can be toxic in certain quantities.

Digging

Dogs love to dig. They find it both necessary and pleasurable. Unfortunately, their idea of fun can cause you a significant amount of frustration and heartache, especially when your precious pooch digs his way to China right under your newly planted rose bushes. If you do not care if your four-legged friend's full-time job is excavating your yard, you have nothing to worry about. Let him dig away, provided, of course, it is safe for him to do so. However, if you prefer not to have potholes in your garden and lawn, prevention is the best solution.

Most dogs dig out of frustration or boredom. Some dig holes to bury their favorite toys or bones. Others dig in order to find a cool spot to escape the heat. Use your imagination to come up with fun games that will stimulate his mind, burn excess energy, and tire him out. For example, purchase a food-dispensing puzzle that allows him to exercise his brain as he tries to outsmart the toy. There are chew toys that can be stuffed with squeeze cheese or peanut butter to provide your Rottweiler with hours of entertainment.

Or, play fun Find It games where you hide a tasty tidbit of food under a box, dish, or bucket and encourage him to find it. Play hide-and-seek games where you encourage him to find you.

If your Rottweiler is digging to find a cool spot to escape the heat, his digging may be the least of your problems. Like many dogs, Rottweilers do not tolerate hot weather. You need to get him

Nylabone®

out of the heat and provide him with a cool spot, such as an air-conditioned room or a cool grassy area with plenty of shade.

Dogs also like to dig in fresh soil and newly fertilized gardens. They are frequently attracted to the smell of chicken and steer manure. The best solution for digging in gardens and flower boxes is prevention. Do not allow your Rottweiler free access to garden areas where he can dig and wreak havoc. An alternative is to install a small fence around the garden, or put chicken wire under the soil so that digging becomes less productive and rewarding for the dog.

Jumping Up

Puppies and adult dogs love to jump on people. It's their way of getting close to your face and greeting you. If you don't mind your dog jumping on you—and some owners don't—then you have nothing to worry about. However, what you think is cute, harmless puppy behavior is far from amusing when your Rottweiler weighs 100 pounds (45.4 kg) and has four muddy feet. An adult dog outweighs most kids and more than a few adults. For this reason alone, you should discourage your dog from jumping.

If you do not want your adult dog to jump on you, do not allow the behavior when he is a puppy.

The key is to discourage all occasions of jumping up. If you do not want your adult dog to jump on you, do not allow the behavior when he is a puppy. It is equally unfair to allow him to jump on you but correct him for jumping on visitors; or to allow him to jump on you today but not tomorrow when you are wearing white pants.

As soon as you see your puppy coming to greet you, crouch down and make a fuss of him. As you do this, slip your thumb in his collar under his chin (your thumb should be pointing down toward the ground) and apply gentle pressure so that he cannot jump up. Give him praise only when all four feet are on the ground. Your praise should be sincere, but not overly enthusiastic. Otherwise, you are likely to wind him up even more.

To prevent your puppy (or adult dog) from jumping on visitors, make sure he is on leash before you open the door. This allows you to control his behavior without grabbing at his collar. When he sits nicely without pawing or mauling your

Tips to Help Prevent Problem Barking

These tips will help enhance your chances of success:
- Consistency and timing are keys to success. You must be consistent each time your dog barks until you can train him to respond to your Quiet or No Bark command.
- Positive reinforcement is much more powerful than negative reinforcement. Verbally praise and reward the behavior you want, which is your dog not barking.
- Dogs learn an appropriate alternative to barking when you are there to teach them. If you are not present to teach them, you cannot expect them to learn on their own.
- Dogs are individuals. They learn at different rates. You may see improvement within a few days — or it may take many weeks.

guests, calmly raise and reward him with a tasty tidbit. "That's my good boy!" Incorporate the entire family by allowing them to practice being a visitor. One at a time, have them go outside, ring the doorbell, then you open the door and invite them in as if they were a visitor. Besides making it a fun family venture, you will eventually have a puppy who grows into an adult dog who does not grope your guests.

Small children like to run, flail their arms, and make loud squealing noises. This type of behavior is especially attractive to young puppies. Most likely, a young child will not be able to control a jumping puppy, let alone a 100-pound (45.4 kg) dog. Therefore, always supervise children and manage your dog so that he is not put in a position where he can develop bad habits.

Running Off or Not Coming when Called

Rottweilers who run away from their owners or refuse to come when called can create an enormous amount of frustration and angst. The good news is that this is one of the easiest problems to solve. The key is to never allow your puppy to develop the bad habit of running off. Each and every time you go outside, your puppy should be on leash. If you want your puppy to run around and explore his surroundings, he should be dragging his leash or a lightweight long-line. If your puppy starts to wander off, simply step on the long-line and reel him back in.

If your adult dog has already developed the annoying habit of running off or ignoring your Come command, a leash or long-line will prevent him from continuing to do so. Then, go back and re-teach him to Come when called. You also should never get in the habit of chasing your puppy, or allowing your kids to chase your puppy. Dogs think this is a fun game, but it teaches a dog to run away from you, which is not only annoying but also dangerous. A puppy or adult dog who runs away from his owner can easily dart into traffic and cause serious injury to himself.

WHEN TO SEEK PROFESSIONAL HELP

Despite your best efforts to raise a well-behaved Rottweiler, undoubtably times arise when things go terribly wrong, and you may need to call in an expert. Some problems, such as aggression and separation anxiety, are complicated areas of canine behavior that require expert guidance. These behaviors are multifaceted and often have overlapping causes. For instance, genetics, lack of socialization, sexual maturity/frustration, lack of obedience training, inappropriate corrections, and pain are a few reasons why dogs might display aggression. Dogs with true separation anxiety issues can work themselves into a heart-racing frenzy. They often become anxious, salivate, pace, whine, bark, and literally freak out to the point of destroying anything and everything they can get their teeth and paws on including couches, walls, doors, rugs, and plants.

If you feel you and your dog need expert advice—don't hesitate to seek it. There is no shame in asking someone who makes their bread and butter training dogs for guidance. You and your dog will be much happier in the long run!

Professionals in the Field

To find the right dog expert, you must first sort through the terminology. Armed with the proper information, you can make an informed and educated decision about which professional is best qualified to help you meet yours and your dog's training goals.

- **Professional dog trainers** and **dog obedience instructors** are often lumped into the same category. A fine line of distinction exists but, for the sake of discussion, they both train dogs. They are hands-on. They utilize practical applications for teaching basic obedience commands; reconditioning and retraining behaviors; and for offering solutions to common problems including aggression, separation anxiety, not coming when called, chewing, digging, jumping up, nipping, and so on. They may teach group obedience classes and/or offer private lessons. Most have dogs, and many are involved in the sport of dogs.

Teething

Around 4 weeks of age, puppies begin to develop their baby teeth—also known as deciduous or milk teeth. Teething is the process of growing baby teeth. The process ends when a dog's permanent teeth are in place. Teething varies from puppy to puppy, with most puppies undergoing some form of continuous teething until they are about 9 months of age. Baby teeth are either erupting or being replaced by permanent teeth. This stimulates an uncontrollable urge to chew as a means of relieving some of the discomfort and as a way to facilitate the removal of their baby teeth.

Many dog obedience instructors focus on puppy training, basic pet obedience, and competitive dog sports, such as obedience, herding, field work, tracking, and so on. They may be members of an organization, such as the National Association of Dog Obedience Instructors. Most trainers learn techniques from other trainers, apprenticeships, academic studies, or a combination.

- **Applied animal behaviorists** have post-graduate degrees in animal behavior, such as biology or zoology. They take scientific knowledge about animal behavior and apply it to real-life issues, such as digging, chewing, barking, jumping, aggression, separation anxiety, and house soiling. Their study is not limited to dogs, and many teach at universities and work in zoos, animal shelters, and research facilities. They may not own a dog, and they may not have ever obedience-trained a dog. Many animal behaviorists consult owners over the telephone for a fee. They generally work one-on-one with the owner, as opposed to group classes.

- **Animal behavior consultants** are similar to applied animal behaviorists but without the post-graduate academic degree. They use knowledge about animal behavior to evaluate, manage, and modify a wide variety of canine behaviors including aggression, separation anxiety, jumping, nipping, and housetraining problems. Many work with other animals including cats, horses, and birds. They may not own a dog, and they may not have ever obedience-trained a dog. Many are certified by organizations such as the International Association of Animal Behavior Consultants (IAABC).

- **Veterinary behaviorists** are veterinarians who have successfully completed the requirements for board certification in the American Veterinary Medical Association (AVMA) veterinary specialty of animal behavior. Veterinary behaviorists are medical experts with a special interest in animal behavior. They work with a number of different animals, including dogs. The American College of Veterinary Behaviorists (ACVB) is the official certifying organization for veterinary behaviorists.

Finding a Behaviorist or Consultant

To find a behaviorist or consultant, start by contacting professional organizations for a referral, such as the American

College of Veterinary Behaviorists, American Veterinary Medical Association, Animal Behavior Society, International Association of Animal Behavior Consultants, or the Association of Pet Behavior Counsellors (United Kingdom).

Also, many universities and colleges have applied animal behaviorists on staff. Contact them for referrals. Ask your vet for a referral, since many behaviorists and consultants work with veterinarians.

What To Look For

Before selecting a behaviorist or consultant, you owe it to yourself, your dog, and your pocketbook to ask important questions and do a bit of research:

- First and foremost, rule out any health issues first by taking your dog to a veterinarian for a thorough examination.
- Once you have located a trainer or behaviorist, call to discuss an appointment, her qualifications and experience, your predicament, and what steps you have taken thus far to resolve the problem.
- Time is money, so don't expect an hour-long free consultation. However, the person should be as equally interested in you and your dog's situation as you are in them.
- Don't be afraid to ask about his training or "modification" techniques. How long has he been working with dogs? What breeds? Does he have "hands-on" experience? Own a dog? Involved in any dog sports?
- Ask about rates, refund policies, and whether other family members can be present.
- Ask for references and contact numbers. If she won't give them to you, find another expert.
- What equipment is required? Some people will try to sell you gadgetry including special collars, leashes, clickers, books, and videotapes.
- Be cautious of anyone who guarantees she can fix any problem. Problem behaviors are managed—not cured. It takes a commitment from both owner and expert.
- Avoid experts who make you feel guilty about the breed you have chosen or your dog's behaviors. If you have created a problem, chances are it was inadvertent.

7

ADVANCED TRAINING AND ACTIVITIES
With Your Rottweiler

Rottweilers are intelligent, energetic, and love to work. They have an excellent desire to please when a strong human–canine bond exists and, because of their strong multipurpose background, Rottweilers can and do succeed in a variety of canine sports. That makes finding the perfect sport or pastime for you and your Rottweiler relatively easy. After all, there are countless canine activities from which to choose! It may take a few tries at different activities, but chances are there is a canine sport—or two!—with your Rottweiler's name on it.

ORGANIZED COMPETITIONS

Training and competing with your Rottweiler allows you to build a strong and mutually respectful relationship and have a great deal of fun in the process. You might even ignite the competitive spark and find yourself hooked on canine competitions. If your Rottweiler is not breed quality, don't worry; you can enter plenty of canine sports that will showcase your dog's agility, athleticism, and intelligence. Through American Kennel Club–sanctioned events alone, you and your Rottweiler can participate in the Canine Good Citizen, Obedience, Rally Obedience, Agility, Tracking, Herding, and Conformation.

Agility

Agility is one of the fastest growing sports for dogs, and one of the most exciting, fast-paced canine sports for spectators. It is an extension of obedience, but without all the formality and precision. Agility courses are more reminiscent of equestrian Grand Prix courses that include assorted jumps and hurdles. In agility, dogs demonstrate their agile nature and versatility by maneuvering through a timed obstacle course of jumps, tunnels, A-frames, weave poles, teeter-totters, ramps, and a pause box. Unlike obedience, agility handlers are permitted to talk to their dogs and even give multiple commands.

A good agility handler is like a navigator. She aims the dog toward each successive obstacle while trying to regulate the dog's speed and precision, and, of course, trying to

Agility Tidbit

In 2004, two Rottweilers earned the prestigious MACH title.

stay the heck out of the way of a fast performing dog. A perfect score in any class is 100, and competitors are faulted if they go over the allotted course time or receive a penalty, such as taking an obstacle out of sequence, missing a contact zone, touching the dog, and so forth.

All-breed agility trials are the most common type of trial, and they are open to all AKC breeds and varieties of dogs. Specialty trials are restricted to dogs of a specific breed or varieties of one breed. Two types of classes are offered at an agility trial: Standard and Jumpers with Weaves. The Standard class has a pause box and contact obstacles—yellow contact zones at each end of the obstacle. The dog must place at least one paw in the contact zone—otherwise, he receives a fault. The goal is to encourage safety in training and in running the course. The Jumpers with Weaves class also has a variety of obstacles, but does not have contact obstacles or a pause box to slow the competitor's forward momentum. Within each agility class are different levels of competition:

- Novice: for the dog just starting in agility. The course contains 13 to 15 obstacles, and the focus is on completing each obstacle with a minimum of handling skill required.
- Open: for the dog who has completed the Novice level. The course contains 16 to 18 obstacles, and the degree of difficultly increases. The Open class also requires significantly more handling skills than the Novice class.
- Excellent: for the dog who has completed the Open level. There are 18 to 20 obstacles, the degree of difficulty increases significantly, and the focus is to provide competitors with the opportunity to demonstrate their superior training, communication, and handling skills.

For the die-hard agility competitor, the Master Agility Champion Title (MACH) is the pinnacle of agility competition. To achieve a

The History of Agility

The origin of Agility can be traced across the Atlantic to Great Britain. The sport originated in 1978, as a small-scale demonstration in the main ring at the prestigious Crufts Dog Show. The show committee wanted an entertainment venue to fill the spare time between the Obedience championships and the Group judging. As a result, John Varley and Peter Meanwell designed a challenging obstacle course, borrowing many elements from equestrian events. The challenging obstacles and fast-paced dogs hooked spectators and the rest, as they say, is history.

Agility courses can include weave poles, jumps, and tunnels.

MACH title, a dog must exhibit speed and consistency on the agility course. He must receive a minimum of 750 champion points and 20 double-qualifying scores from the Excellent B Standard and Excellent B Jumpers and Weaves class. To put it in layman terms, handlers receive one champion point for each full second under the standard course time. They can double the championship points received if they place first in their class. It is challenging, but not impossible for the Rottweiler owner. The best way to get started in agility is to join a local dog-training club or visit an agility training facility.

Herding

Herding trials are designed to develop and preserve the droving skills inherent in the herding breeds and to demonstrate that they can perform the useful functions for which they were originally bred. Despite the breed's classification in the AKC Working Group, the Rottweiler's background as a cattle herding and drover dog allows him to participate in the AKC herding tests and trials. While these tests and trials are artificial simulations of working pastoral or farm conditions, they do provide a standardized test by which owners can measure their dog's inherent herding abilities and training.

The AKC herding program has two major divisions: Herding Tests and Herding Trials.

Herding Tests are noncompetitive tests intended for dogs with little or no prior herding experience. Dogs must, however, show a sustained interest in herding livestock. Within this division, owners can earn two certifications: HT (Herding Tested Dog), which indicates a dog has shown herding instinct and is under basic control, and a PT

Canine Good Citizen

If you enjoy training your Rottweiler, but organized competitions are not your cup of tea, the American Kennel Club's Canine Good Citizen (CGC) program might be a viable alternative. Implemented in 1989, the CGC program is a public education and certification program designed to demonstrate that the dog, as a companion to man, can be a respected member of the community. The CGC program encourages owners to develop a positive and worthwhile relationship with their dogs by rewarding responsible dog ownership and good pet manners. It is designed to encourage owners to get involved with and obedience-train their dogs.

While the program does not involve the formality or precision of competitive obedience, it does lay the foundation for good pet manners and is often used as a stepping stone for other canine activities, such as obedience, rally obedience, and agility. Owners can help combat negative opinions about the Rottweiler by training and readying their dog for this relatively simple test.

The CGC program is a noncompetitive, ten-part test that evaluates your Rottweiler's behavior in practical situations at home, in public, and in the presence of unfamiliar people and other dogs. The pass or fail test is designed to test a Rottweiler's reaction to distractions, friendly strangers, and supervised isolation. Additionally, a Rottweiler must sit politely while being petted, walk on a loose leash, walk through a crowd, and respond to basic obedience commands including Sit, Down, Stay, and Come. The evaluator also inspects the dog to determine if he is clean and groomed. Both purebred and mixed-breed dogs are eligible to participate. While there is no age limit, dogs must be old enough to have received their immunizations.

(Pretrial Tested Dog), which indicates that a dog and handler worked together as a team, and the dog had a modest amount of training but not enough to compete in the lowest level trial.

Herding Trials are competitive trials intended for dogs with substantial training. Dogs must demonstrate the ability to move and control livestock. The titles awarded in each division are: HS Herding Started, HI Herding Intermediate, HX Herding Excellent, and H CH Champion. For an H CH, a dog must have earned an HX and at least 15 championship points in the advanced classes.

Obedience

Every aspect of dog ownership involves some form of obedience training, yet the obedience ring seldom receives the PR and media attention of other canine events. An obedience competition goes well beyond the CGC program and tests a Rottweiler's ability to perform a prescribed set of exercises in a formal environment. One might compare it to the formal and elegant equine dressage tests, in which owners achieve a harmonious relationship with their dogs, all the while observing meticulous attention to minute details.

The three levels of competitive obedience are:

- The Novice Level: The dog is required to heel on and off leash at a normal, fast, and slow pace; come when called; stand for a physical examination by the judge; and do a sit-stay and a down-stay with other dogs. Other than giving commands, handlers are not allowed to talk to their dog during the exercise, nor are they allowed to use toys, treats, or other training aids in the ring. Dogs who complete this level receive a Companion Dog (CD) title.

- The Open Level: The Open class is quite a bit more difficult than the Novice class because all exercises are performed off leash. A dog is required to do heel-work exercises similar to those in the Novice class, as well as a retrieve exercise, a drop on recall, a high jump, broad jump, and a sit-stay and a down-stay with other dogs while the handlers are out of sight. Dogs who complete this level receive a Companion Dog Excellent (CDX) title.

- The Utility Level: Utility is the final and most difficult and challenging level of training. The exercises include scent discrimination, directed jumping, retrieving, hand signals, and a moving stand and examination. Completing this level awards your dog a Utility Dog (UD) title.

If you've gotten this far, you are seriously committed to the sport of obedience, and you may decide to work toward a Utility Dog Excellent (UDX) or Obedience Trial Championship title (OTCH)—the créme de la créme of obedience competition. While it is considered the most prestigious title, it has also proven to be the most elusive crown since its inception in 1977.

The best way to get involved in obedience is to sign up for a dog obedience class or join a local dog obedience club. If you are interested in the sport of competitive obedience, find a trainer who competes in the sport and teaches competitive obedience classes.

Herding Tidbit

In 2004, 53 Rottweilers earned their HT titles; 36 Rottweilers earned their PT titles; 17 Rottweilers earned HS titles; 10 Rottweilers earned HI titles, and 3 Rottweilers earned HX titles.

Rally Obedience

Rally obedience is the newest AKC event—a combination of agility and obedience. However, the emphasis is less on speed and precision and more on how well dogs and handlers perform together as a team. It was created with the average dog owner in mind and as a means to help promote a positive human–canine relationship, with an emphasis on fun and excitement. It also takes the pressure off competing, while still allowing owners to showcase their Rottweilers' obedience skills.

In rally obedience, the dog and handler move through a course designed by the rally judge, proceeding at their own pace through a

course of between 10 and 20 stations, depending on the level. Each of these stations has a sign providing instructions regarding the skill to be performed, such as Halt & Sit; Halt, Sit, & Down, and the like.

Unlike traditional obedience competitions, handlers are permitted to talk to their dog, use praise, clap their hands, pat their legs, or use any verbal means of communication and body language throughout the performance. Handlers may not touch their dog or make physical corrections. Any dog who is eligible for AKC registration can enter Rally obedience.

Showing (Conformation)

Conformation shows (dog shows) are the signature events of the competitive dog world. The conformation ring, commonly referred to as the breed ring, provides a forum for breeders and handlers to showcase the best in breeding stock. These animals are evaluated as potential breeding stock and usually are incorporated into future breeding programs in an effort to improve the breed. For this reason, dogs competing in conformation may not be spayed or neutered.

How Dog Shows Work

The best way to understand the conformation ring is to think of it in terms of an elimination process. Each Rottweiler enters a regular class and is evaluated against the Rottweiler breed standard. For the newcomer, it often appears as if the dogs are competing against one another. And, in a sense they are. However, the judge is not comparing the quality of one Rottweiler against the quality of another Rottweiler. The judge is evaluating each Rottweiler against the breed standard and how closely each dog measures up to the ideal Rottweiler, as outlined in the breed standard.

The regular classes are divided by sex, with the male and female dogs being judged separately. The male dogs are always judged first, and after being examined by the judge they are placed first through fourth according to how well they measure up to the Rottweiler breed standard in the judge's opinion. After the males have been judged, the females go through the same judging process.

After the regular classes have been judged, the first-place winners of each class are brought back to the ring to compete against one another in the Winners Class. The dog selected is the Winners Dog and is awarded championship points. A Reserve Winners Dog also is chosen but does not receive points unless the

Benched Shows

Conformation shows are either benched or unbenched. At a benched show, dogs are grouped together by breed in a central area and are on display during the entire show, except for grooming, exercising, and showing. A benched show is an educational venue that allows spectators to view, admire, and learn about dog breeds in an up-close and controlled surrounding. While a few shows remain benched—including the prestigious Westminster Kennel Club show—the majority of shows today are unbenched. Dogs may be kept anywhere when not showing, and you are not required to stay on the show grounds after you show your dog.

Winners Dog, for any reason, is disallowed or disqualified. The same process is then repeated with the female dogs, resulting in a Winners Bitch and Reserve Winners Bitch.

The Winners Dog and Winners Bitch go back into the ring with any Champions entered to compete for the Best of Breed award. If either the Winners Dog or Winners Bitch wins Best of Breed or Best of Winners, they may also win more points. The Best of Breed dog or bitch then goes on to the Group. The Group winners are then judged with Group placements—first through fourth—being awarded in each of the seven groups. The first-place Group winners compete for the most coveted and most prestigious award: Best in Show.

Earning a Championship

To attain an AKC Championship title, each Rottweiler must win a total of 15 points. Only the Winners Dog and Winners Bitch receive points. The number of points earned at each show is predetermined by a point schedule that varies from region to region.

The number of points awarded at each show depends on the breed, the number of dogs entered in the competition, and the location of the show. For example, points awarded to a Rottweiler in New York will differ from the number of points awarded in California. The number of points that can be won at a show is between one and five. Three-, four-, and five-point wins are considered majors. One- and two-point wins are considered minors. Of the 15 points required for a Championship title, six or more of the points must be majors. The remaining points may be attained in any combination, including major or minor wins, but must be won under different judges than the two major wins. So you need to win points under at least three different judges. A Rottweiler can add to the number of points he won in the Winners Class if he also wins Best of Breed, Best of Opposite Sex, or Best of

Winners. Once the requirements are met and officially confirmed, then a championship certificate is issued for the individual dog.

Showing Your Rottweiler

Dog showing is a gratifying and rewarding way to meet new people, spend countless hours with your Rottweiler, and build a strong human–canine bond. However, dog showing, like most sports, is an art that must be learned and practiced regularly. If you are interested in conformation shows, you will need to learn to groom, condition, and present your Rottweiler in the best possible light. You will need to learn about the structure and movement of Rottweilers. You will need to dress appropriately—not so flashy that you detract from your dog, but not so casual that you look like you came straight from mucking stalls. You will need proper shoes that provide comfort and are suitable for running. There are so many things of which you will have no control—the weather, judging schedules, bitches that come into season, schedules that move slower than you like, but you can control how you and your dog are represented and presented in the ring.

Regardless of the event, you must have a thorough understanding and comprehension of the rules and regulations governing the show. You should obtain a copy of the rules and regulations for the governing organization, such as AKC, CKC, KC, or UKC, and read it thoroughly.

The best way to get involved in showing dogs is to attend shows and ask a lot of questions. Most dog people are more than willing

In dog shows, judges look for how closely each dog measures up to the ideal Rottweiler as outlined in the breed standard.

Three Types of Conformation Shows

- All-breed shows are exactly what the name implies. They are open to over 150 breeds and varieties of dogs recognized by the American Kennel Club, and include shows such as the prestigious Westminster Kennel Club. These are the conformation shows you are most likely to see on television.
- Specialty shows are for one specific breed, such as the Rottweiler. Most often, local, regional, or national breed-specific clubs sponsor these shows.
- Group shows are limited to dogs belonging to one of the seven groups. For example, a working group show would feature only breeds belonging to the working group.

to help the newcomer. If possible, join a local dog club, and find a mentor, such as a Rottweiler breeder or professional handler who is willing to help you maneuver the ins and outs of dog shows.

Tracking

The first AKC licensed tracking test took place on June 13, 1936. Today, tracking is a popular sport that tests a Rottweiler's ability to recognize and track a human scent over varying terrains and climatic changes. It is designed to showcase a dog's intelligence and extremely high level of scent capability. The goal is for the dog to follow a scented track and locate an article left at the end of the trail by a tracklayer.

Rottweilers can earn three different tracking titles: Tracking Dog (TD), Tracking Dog Excellent (TDX), and Variable Surface Tracking (VST). If a Rottweiler successfully completes all three tracking titles, he earns the prestigious title of Champion Tracker (CT).

For a Rottweiler to earn a TD title, the dog must follow a track 440 to 500 yards (402.3 to 457.2 m), with three to five changes of direction, and the track must be aged at least 30 minutes but not more than 2 hours before the dog can begin scenting (following the track).

A TDX title is the next level and slightly more difficult than a TD. It is earned when a Rottweiler follows a track between 800 and 1,000 yards (731.5 to 914.4 m) and between 3 and 5 hours old. The TDX track must have five to seven directional changes and also includes the additional challenge of human cross tracks, which, as the name implies, is a human track that crosses the primary track. A dog must also locate four articles rather than the one article required for a TD.

TD and TDX tracks are laid through open fields and wilderness areas and include varying terrain conditions, such as gullies, plowed land, woods, and vegetation. However, urban sprawl has

severely limited those spaces in some parts of the country. As a result, the Variable Surface Tracking (VST) title was designed to utilize industrial and office parks, college campuses, and so forth. To earn a VST title, dogs must first have a TD title, and must follow a track of 600 to 800 yards (548.6 to 731.5 m) in length and between 3 to 5 hours old. The track may take them down a street, between buildings, across a college campus, asphalt parking lot, concrete sidewalk, and the like.

Unlike obedience and agility titles that require a dog and handler to qualify three times, a Rottweiler only needs to complete one track successfully to earn each title. If you and your Rottweiler love the great outdoors, tracking might be the sport for you. The best way to get involved in tracking is to contact a local dog obedience club or a national organization, such as the American Rottweiler Club, American Kennel Club, The Kennel Club, or Canadian Kennel Club.

OTHER FUN SPORTS

Carting

Carting allows you to showcase your Rottweiler's cart pulling capabilities, which historically was a valued function of the breed. Rottweiler owners have been carting in parades unofficially for many years. For added fun, teach your Rottweiler to pull one or two small kids in a two- or four-wheeled cart. Harness your Rottweiler's desire to work while channeling his excess energy by having him help with chores around the house—pulling a cart filled with gardening tools or yard debris, hauling firewood, pulling trash cans to the curb, or hauling the Christmas tree in from the woods. His carting capabilities are limited only by your imagination.

If you want to take carting to a more competitive level, you can enter carting competitions and earn carting titles. Carting competitions are designed to demonstrate a dog's carting abilities, training skills, and strength and endurance, with emphasis on a team effort by both dog and handler.

As with all canine activities, it is prudent to make sure your Rottweiler is physically capable of hauling a cart. He should be in good physical condition—not over- or underweight—with no underlying health problems, such as hip or elbow dysplasia. Always start slowly and progress at a level conducive to your dog's

Showing in the United Kingdom

Earning a breed championship in England is quite a bit different than in the United States because they do not have a point system. Challenge Certificates (CC) are awarded if the judge feels the dog is deserving regardless of the number of dogs in competition. A dog becomes a Show Champion (Sh Ch) when he has been awarded three Challenge Certificates under three different judges, provided at least one of the CC's was awarded after the age of 12 months. Challenge Certificates are only available at championship shows and competition is extremely strong because entries are usually quite large and dogs trying to win a CC and earn a championship have to beat several champions to gain the title.

In England, the Kennel Club also requires that certain dogs (i.e., Gundog Breeds and Border Collies), qualify in a working capacity before becoming a Champion. The title of Champion (CH) is awarded once a dog has met the Show Champion requirements and passed the working test.

If they do not qualify in the working aspect, they are designated a Show Champion, which is equivalent to the AKC's Champion of Record.

individual physical and mental capabilities. If your Rottweiler is younger than 2 years, you will need to take special care not to injure his growing bones and ligaments. A good rule of thumb is to limit the amount of weight he pulls to no more than one-tenth of his body weight.

The most important piece of equipment you need is the harness. A proper-fitting harness will help prevent injuries to your Rottweiler—so don't skimp on quality. It should be specially designed for carting or drafting. Carts come in a variety of sizes, including two- and four-wheeled. Safety and maneuverability are always important factors to consider when choosing a cart. Do your homework and research what is best for your dog.

Most organizations do not permit dogs to compete until they are 18 months to 2 years old. The American Kennel Club does not sanction carting events or offer carting titles. However, the Canadian Kennel Club does offer Draft Dog titles, including a Draft Dog, Draft Dog Excellent, Brace Draft Dog, and Brace Draft Dog Excellent titles.

Flyball

Invented in the late 1970s, Flyball is yet another exhilarating choice in the list of entertaining sports you can do with your Rottweiler. It is the sport for all tennis ball–loving dogs! To say Flyball is fast-paced is an understatement. It is a high-octane relay race that showcases a Rottweiler's speed and agility. Don't worry—your Rottweiler does all the running in this sport! It is a team sport rather than an individual competition, and an equally thrilling and entertaining spectator sport.

The course consists of four hurdles (small jumps) spaced approximately 10 feet (3 m) apart. Fifteen feet beyond the last hurdle is a spring-loaded box that contains a tennis ball. Just as in any relay race, the fastest team to successfully complete the game wins. The goal is for each dog to take a turn running the relay by leaping each of the four hurdles and then hitting a pedal or lever with his paw to trigger the box, which shoots a tennis ball up in the air. Once the dog catches the ball in his mouth, he races back over the four hurdles to the finish line, where the next dog is anxiously awaiting his turn.

The first team to have all four dogs run without errors wins the heat. If a dog misses a hurdle or fails to retrieve the ball, he must repeat his turn. For additional information contact the North American Flyball Association or the British Flyball Association.

Skijoring

In its simplest terms, skijoring is being pulled on skis by one or more dogs in harness. The great thing about skijoring is that almost any dog (over 30 pounds) can participate, which makes it ideal for the athletic Rottweiler. With a minimum amount of equipment, an eager Rottweiler, and a pair of cross- country skis, you can have the time of your life—while increasing the human–canine bond.

Skijoring is fairly easy to learn, but it does require some basic skills. You must be somewhat proficient on cross-country skis, your Rottweiler must be accustomed to wearing a harness, and he must know how to pull. It is helpful if your dog has some basic obedience skills, as well. It's fun, exhilarating, and the perfect canine sport if you and your Rottweiler enjoy the great outdoors.

Weight-Pull

Canine weight-pull competitions are not unlike tractor pull competitions—except the dogs do all the work. It is a natural extension of carting, and the powerful Rottweiler is a natural for both sports!

In weight-pull competitions, dogs compete within their individual weight class to see which dog can pull the most weight over 16 feet (4.8 m). A dog can pull a weighted sled on snow or a wheeled cart on a natural surface, and the weight is gradually increased until one dog remains. Ties are decided based on the dogs' times from the previous round.

As with carting, dogs wear specially designed harnesses that disperse tension and reduce the possibility of injury. Dogs excel at this venue because they love to work—not because they are being forced to pull. As with all canine activities, start slowly and progress at a rate suitable for the mental and physical capabilities of your dog. Dogs must be 2 years old to compete in weight pulls sanctioned by the International Weight Pulling Association, but they can begin light training around 18 months of age.

While the AKC does not sanction weight-pulling competitions, titles are available through a number of dog clubs and organizations including the United Kennel Club and the International Weight Pull Association (IWPA).

OTHER ACTIVITIES

Swimming

Swimming is an excellent activity for cooling off, burning calories, and sharing quality time with your Rottweiler. Be forewarned: Not all Rottweilers take to the water like, well, a fish to water. You may need to take it slowly and introduce your Rottweiler to water playfully and gradually. It is never advisable to toss your young Rottweiler into the water. It is highly likely that doing so will frighten him—not to mention the possibility of injuring him and turning him off to swimming and water activities for the rest of his life.

For the reluctant Rottweiler, try to find a swimming pool, lake, or shallow pond that has a gentle sloping bank. Kiddy pools or wading pools are also excellent for the hesitant swimmer. Encourage your Rottweiler to wade in with you or throw a floatable toy for him to retrieve, being careful in the beginning to toss it close to the bank of the pond or edge of the pool. If you toss it too far, it is likely he will find the task of retrieving too daunting.

The ocean is wonderful for invigorating walks on the beach and dips in the ocean. Your Rottweiler may be content to dip his feet in the foam. Or he

Once your Rottweiler is comfortable with basic commands, you can start to get involved in many fun sports.

Carting, Drafting, and Driving

To get involved in carting, you will need to know what the terms mean:

- Carting is defined as pulling a two- or four-wheeled cart (or vehicle) with or without passengers.

- Drafting is pulling a vehicle without a passenger.

- Driving refers to carting in which the handler rides in the vehicle being pulled by the dog.

may be more adventurous and take a full body plunge. It is important to keep your Rottweiler close to shore, regardless of his superior athleticism and swimming capabilities. Riptides and undercurrents are unpredictable, and your Rottweiler can quickly wade into trouble.

Most dogs will play until they exhaust themselves and collapse into a heap of sleep. Therefore, it is important to watch for signs that your dog is getting tired, such as slowing down or slapping the water with his front feet. A lifejacket designed specifically for dogs may give you some peace of mind while providing a safety net for your water-loving companion.

Walking, Jogging, Hiking

The Rottweiler is a natural trotter and, if built correctly and conditioned properly, he can trot for long distances. As a result, Rotties make excellent exercise companions and, no doubt, both you and your Rottweiler will benefit from the exercise and companionship. It is worth reiterating that hot weather bothers Rottweilers. Therefore, if you plan to include your Rottweiler in your daily walks or jogs, limit these activities to cooler parts of the day, such as the early morning or evening. Equally important, hot sidewalks and roads can burn a Rottweiler's feet, causing an enormous amount of pain and discomfort. If the sidewalks and roadways are too hot for your bare feet, they are too hot for your Rottweiler's feet.

How far a Rottweiler can walk, jog, or hike, depends on his age, physical condition, the terrain covered, and the weather. An extended hike through rough terrain and rocky surfaces may be a piece of cake for the conditioned dogs, but too taxing for some canine couch potatoes. Always carry plenty of fluid for both you and your Rottweiler.

CANINE CAREERS

The terms *therapy dogs* and *service dogs* often are used interchangeably. However, a significant difference exists. The Americans with Disabilities Act uses the term Service Dog to define a dog who has been "individually trained to work or perform tasks for the benefit of a person with a disability." Professionals within the industry often refer to them as Assistance Dogs, rather than Service Dogs. Therapy dogs provide companionship and emotional support, but do not perform tasks, and federal law does not legally define them.

Sports and Safety

Before beginning any physically challenging activity with your Rottweiler, take him to the veterinarian's for a thorough check-up and examination. Joint problems, such as hip and elbow dysplasia, are common in some Rottweilers and should be of paramount concern for owners. They may preclude your Rottweiler from some of the more physically demanding activities. Low-stress activities are wonderful for puppies, but young dogs (generally under the age of 2 years) should not be allowed to jump. Too much pressure on developing joints and limbs can injure your puppy and lead to lifelong problems.

Four categories of dog are recognized under the umbrella of Assistance Dogs: therapy dogs, guide dogs, service dogs, and hearing dogs. The last three categories usually employ Golden Retrievers, Labrador Retrievers, or German Shepherds. You rarely see a Rottweiler performing those types of services. But if your Rottweiler has the right temperament, you may want to explore the area of therapy work.

Therapy Dogs

Therapy is an important area in which Rottweilers can help enhance the humane–canine bond by providing unconditional love, companionship, and emotional support to nursing home, hospital, assisted living, and mental health residents. Owners volunteering with their Rottweilers make regularly scheduled visits and brighten the lives of residents by providing stimulation, companionship, and a vehicle for conversation and interaction.

A word of caution: Rottweilers are big and strong, and even the sweetest tempered Rottweiler can be intimidating. Only Rottweilers who are well mannered and have a sound temperament should undertake this work. While it is personally satisfying to see how dogs can brighten the lives of residents, 90 percent of the work is done by the dogs, and they must have the physical and mental fortitude to cope with strange noises and smells, distractions, and often erratic behaviors. Additionally, dogs must be willing to accept a considerable amount of attention, petting, and touching from strangers. It helps if your Rottweiler has a foundation of basic obedience training or his CGC certificate. While the AKC does offer CGC certifications, they do not certify therapy dogs. Independent organizations do exist to certify therapy dogs.

Rotties as Therapy Dogs

Even a burly-looking Rottweiler can make an excellent therapy dog, but only if he is properly trained and has a suitable temperament.

HEALTH
of Your Rottweiler

Like good-quality nutrition, there is no substitute for regular veterinary care. Any number of infectious diseases, parasites, and serious ailments can impair your Rottweiler's health, but today's veterinarians have the academic training and expertise necessary to reduce and prevent serious illnesses, helping to keep your Rottweiler in the best health possible.

CHOOSING A VETERINARIAN

It is never too early to begin looking for a veterinarian. If your new Rottweiler has yet to arrive at your home, or you have recently moved, find a veterinarian before you actually need one. When your Rottweiler is sick or injured, you don't want to be scanning the yellow pages. Just as you spent a great deal of time and energy finding the right Rottweiler for you, invest time and energy in finding a suitable veterinarian with whom you and your precious pooch will feel comfortable and can build a mutually trusting and respectful relationship.

Think about what you want in a veterinarian. Perhaps proximity to your house or work is paramount, or maybe you prefer a small clinic run by one or two doctors. Perhaps you like the idea of a big clinic with access to multiple doctors. Possibly a mobile veterinarian who makes house calls is more to your liking.

A number of different veterinary practices exist, the most common being small-animal practices where veterinarians work mainly with dogs and cats, and occasionally reptiles, ferrets, and birds. Often, these veterinarians will make house calls under special circumstances, such as to euthanize a sick or aging dog.

In rural areas, it is not unusual to see mixed-animal practices, where veterinarians work with dogs and cats, as well as large animals including horses, llamas, and other farm animals. Some veterinarians have mobile practices—a van or truck stocked with medical supplies—and, like doctors of years gone by, they make house calls to treat your Rottweiler.

Some veterinarians specialize in a particular field and are board certified, such as internal

medicine, ophthalmology, radiology, dentistry, dermatology, orthopedics, cardiology, acupuncture, and chiropractic care. A veterinarian who is board certified has studied and passed board-certification exams in that specialty.

How to Find a Veterinarian

Finding the right veterinarian is not difficult, but it can be a bit time consuming. The good news is the hard work you invest today will pay off in the future when you need to put your Rottweiler's health and well-being in the hands of a veterinarian.

To start your search:

- Ask your Rottweiler's breeder for a referral. Most reputable breeders know several local veterinarians and specialists.
- Ask friends, family, neighbors, and colleagues who own a pet for a referral.
- Ask around at local dog clubs, obedience schools, dog groomers, or boarding kennels. These people are usually involved in dogs and will have established a relationship with one or more local veterinarians.
- Local telephone directories are often a good starting point. They give you the names, addresses, and telephone numbers of veterinary and emergency clinics in your area.
- If you are moving from one area to another, ask your current veterinarian to refer you to some veterinarians in your new town.

Visiting the Clinic

You may feel less anxious if you see where your Rottweiler will be spending the day if he needs to be hospitalized overnight or kept for several hours. When visiting veterinary clinics, don't be afraid to ask for a tour of their exam rooms, x-ray room, operating and recovery rooms, boarding areas, and so forth. If the clinic is busy, schedule an appointment, which is not an unreasonable request. If the staff or veterinarians refuse to show you their facilities, run—don't walk—to the nearest exit.

Questions to Ask when Visiting a Clinic

Don't be afraid to ask questions when visiting a clinic—it's the best way to find a place you'll be comfortable and confident taking your Rottweiler.

- What are the regular office hours?

- How are emergencies handled during business hours?
- What about after hours, holidays, and weekends?
- What type of services do they offer—surgeries, hip or elbow x-rays, ultrasound, dentistry, eye exams, endoscopy?
- If they do not offer a service, will they refer you to a specialist?
- Is the veterinarian familiar with the Rottweiler breed?
- Can you see a specific doctor if they are a multidoctor clinic?

Veterinarians, Staff, and Assistants

Like human doctors, veterinarians differ in their bedside manners. No matter how qualified the veterinarian is, if you do not like her or the staff, you will not be comfortable taking your Rottweiler there. The relationship between you and your veterinarian can last for many, many years. Good communication with the doctor and staff is a necessity. Here are some things to consider about the staff at the clinic:

Find a suitable veterinarian with whom you and your precious pooch will feel comfortable.

- Are you comfortable talking with the veterinarian and asking questions?
- Does she seem knowledgeable and friendly?
- Is she patient? Willing to answer your questions? Responsive to your concerns?
- Does she explain the diagnosis, treatment, and expected outcome in layman's terms? Will that be explained again if you don't understand?
- Do you feel rushed?
- Is your Rottweiler treated with kindness, respect, and concern?
- Is the staff knowledgeable, courteous, and friendly? Are they willing to answer your questions and accommodate reasonable requests? Or do they give you the brush off?

Of course, there is always the chance that you will not like a particular veterinarian despite her glowing recommendations, professional reputation in the community, and stellar academic qualifications. If this is the case, keep looking until you find the veterinarian who is right for you.

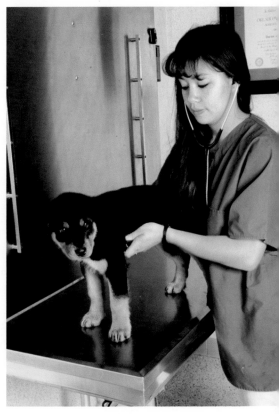

Anyone who has ever owned a dog knows that emergencies never happen between 8 a.m. and 5 p.m. It's Murphy's Law with a twist. Anything that can go wrong will go wrong, and it will happen on weekends, holidays, and always after your veterinarian's office has just closed for the day. Therefore, it is always prudent to know the location of the closest emergency veterinary clinic that can handle emergencies occurring outside your veterinarian's regular office hours. Most generally, they do not handle routine check-ups, vaccinations, or spaying and neutering. Emergency clinics may also see animals that need 24-hour care or exams with specialized equipment that veterinarians in the surrounding area do not have at their facilities.

PREVENTIVE CARE FOR YOUR ROTTWEILER

Once you have found a veterinarian, and you are happy and confident with your choice, it is time to get your Rottweiler an appointment. Generally speaking, get your new pooch to the veterinarian within 48 to 72 hours after acquiring him. This visit establishes a record of health. To the untrained eye, a puppy or adult dog can appear healthy but may have a serious problem. One of the most important and kindest deeds you can do for your Rottweiler is to work with a veterinarian to develop a preventive healthcare plan and schedule routine visits.

The Physical Exam

Your veterinarian will check your Rottweiler's overall condition, which includes inspecting his skin, coat, eyes, ears, feet, lymph nodes, glands, teeth, and gums. He will listen to his heart and lungs, and feel his abdomen, muscles, and joints. Most likely, he will ask you about your puppy's eating and elimination habits. If necessary, jot down any relevant information before going to the vet's, so that you will have it at your fingertips, such as the type of food your puppy eats; how much and how often he eats; how often he relieves himself; the color, shape and size of his stools; and so forth. He will no doubt discuss with you a preventative healthcare plan that includes vaccinations, worming, spaying or neutering, and the scheduling of routine veterinary visits.

Annual Check-ups

You may not feel older from one birthday to the next, but 1 year is a long time in your Rottweiler's life. In a relatively short period, about 7 years, your Rottweiler will have grown from a tiny puppy to a senior citizen. In dog circles, a lot can happen in the span of 1 year, and that is why it is important to schedule (and keep!) annual check-ups for you dog. It is not unusual for owners to inadvertently overlook their Rottweiler's health. Let's face it: How many people go to the doctor's unless they are feeling particularly ill? When your Rottweiler is happy and healthy and full of zest, annual preventative healthcare visits can get overlooked.

Yearly checkups are especially important as your Rottweiler matures. Just as dogs age faster than humans, their diseases progress more quickly, too. Older dogs are more likely to develop problems with their hearing, smell, and sight—not to mention a potpourri of aches, pains, and stiff joints. Aging dogs are also more likely to develop diabetes, kidney problems, and hormonal diseases. Yearly check-ups help your veterinarian to prevent diseases by catching them early on, thereby keeping your Rottweiler healthy well into his senior years.

Spaying and Neutering

A lot of owners have an aversion to spaying or neutering their Rottweiler. Rest assured, your dog will not care one iota that he is neutered. He won't get fat—unless you let him. He won't hate you. He won't hold a grudge. He won't be less of a companion, and, contrary to public opinion, he won't even know his "parts" are missing. Females will not make better pets simply because they have been allowed to whelp "just one litter." In fact, quite the opposite is true. Spaying and neutering will help your Rottweiler to live a longer and healthier life. It's as simple as that.

Advantages for Females
- Spaying helps to reduce or eliminate breast cancer—especially if a female is spayed before her first heat cycle.
- Spaying eliminates the incidence of ovarian and uterine infection or cancer.
- It helps to reduce or prevent mammary gland tumors—the most common tumor in unsprayed females dogs.
- Spaying prevents the nervousness, irritability, and aggressiveness that many females show while in season.

- It eliminates "false pregnancies"—a condition in which a female thinks she is pregnant because of abnormal hormonal changes.
- It eliminates the possibility of passing on genetic defects, such as hip dysplasia and epilepsy.
- It eliminates a female's heat cycle and any possibility of an "accidental" breeding, resulting in unwanted puppies that contribute to pet overpopulation problems.

Advantages for Males

- Neutering eliminates testicular cancer and decreases the incidence of prostate disease. (More than 80 percent of unneutered dogs develop prostate disease.)
- It helps to decrease aggression toward other male dogs, as well as people.
- Some males can sense female "pheromones" as far as 1 mile away. Neutering decreases a dog's desire to "roam" the neighborhood, which in turn reduces the risk of fights, injury, poisoning, accidents, and diseases.
- Neutered dogs have an increased ability to pay attention to their owner because they are not constantly distracted by females in season.
- Neutering eliminates the ability to reproduce and pass on undesired genetic traits, such as hip dysplasia and epilepsy.

Unless you are showing your dog in the show ring or he is part of a designed breeding program, have your dog spayed or neutered as early as possible. While the majority of dogs are altered around 6 months of age, many veterinarians alter dogs as young as 8 weeks of age. Once considered controversial, early spay/neuter procedures are becoming more common. Your veterinarian is the best person to advise you on what age to alter your dog.

VACCINATIONS

The sooner your Rottweiler puppy starts his course of vaccinations, the sooner he will be able to get out and about and begin socializing with people and other animals and exploring his new world. A reputable breeder will most likely have administered a series of vaccinations for distemper, hepatitis, leptospirosis, parvovirus, and parainfluenza, prior to you acquiring your Rottweiler.

Vaccinations are generally first given at 6 to 8 weeks of age and are repeated every 3 to 4 weeks until the puppy is 16 weeks old. You should have received a copy of his vaccination and deworming schedule when you picked up your Rottweiler puppy. It is a good idea to take a copy of your puppy's vaccination schedule with you on your first visit to the veterinarian. Your veterinarian will set up a continued vaccination schedule for your Rottweiler, including a rabies vaccination at the appropriate time. Veterinarians differ on their vaccination protocol, so ask questions, especially if you have any concerns.

Diseases to Vaccinate Against

The following is a list of viral and bacterial diseases for which vaccinations may be recommended for your Rottweiler. Your veterinarian can help you make a decision that takes into account your lifestyle and the region in which you live.

Distemper

Distemper is a highly contagious viral disease that is very similar to the virus that causes measles in humans. It can spread rapidly through kennels or multiple-dog households, especially if unvaccinated dogs are present. Distemper is spread through the air as well as through contact with an infected animal's stool or urine. It is a primary cause of illness and death in unvaccinated puppies.

Dogs of any age can be affected; however, most are puppies less than 6 months of age. Distemper attacks a wide range of canine organs including the skin, brain, eyes, respiratory, digestive, and nervous systems. Symptoms usually appear within 10 to 14 days after exposure. A Rottweiler with distemper may develop nasal and eye discharge, coughing, diarrhea, vomiting, and seizures. Puppies who recover may develop severe enamel damage on their teeth, retinal damage, seizures, and muscular twitches. They may also have nose and footpads that become thickened, hence the name *hardpad disease.* As with most viral diseases, there is no specific medication that will kill the distemper virus. Infected pets are

At the Vet's

During an annual visit, your veterinarian will review important aspects of your dog's health, including:
• Overall health including weight, coat and skin condition, ears, eyes, feet, bones, muscles, as well as neurological and respiratory functions.
• Nutritional requirements.
• Exercise, including how often, what types, changes in ability etc.
• Vaccination requirements.
• Parasite control including fleas, ticks, heartworms, and the like.
• Dental health, such as mouth odors, pain, broken teeth, and related diseases.
• Blood tests for older dogs, those with medical conditions, and those receiving medications.
• Changes in temperament and normal behaviors, problems with barking, chewing, digging, etc.

treated with supportive care including IV fluids, anti-diarrheals, and other medications.

Hepatitis

Hepatitis, also known as canine adenovirus, typically affects the liver, tonsils, and larynx, but can also attack other organs in the body. Initial symptoms include a sore throat, coughing, and occasionally pneumonia. As it enters a Rottweiler's bloodstream, it can affect the liver, kidneys, and the appearance of the eyes, which may become cloudy or bluish. More advanced symptoms are characterized by seizures, increased, thirst, vomiting, and diarrhea. The virus is spread primarily through direct contact with an infected dog, and infected fluids including saliva, nasal discharge, and urine. Rottweilers who were infected but have since recovered can still pass the virus for up to 9 months in their urine. Unvaccinated Rottweilers of all ages are at risk. However, the disease is most prevalent in dogs less than 1 year of age. Like distemper, your veterinarian may use a supportive treatment like IV fluids to help.

Kennel Cough

Kennel cough, also known as canine infectious tracheobronchitis or Bordetellosis, results from an inflammation of a dog's upper airways. Highly contagious, the respiratory disease is normally characterized by a harsh, dry coughing or hacking, which may be followed by retching and gagging. The disease is airborne—meaning it is passed through the air—and can spread rapidly among dogs who live together. While kennel cough is a serious problem, it is not normally fatal unless a secondary infection, such as pneumonia, develops. In severe infections, discharges from the nose and mouth occur along with depression, lack of energy, and loss of appetite. Treatment may include antibiotics.

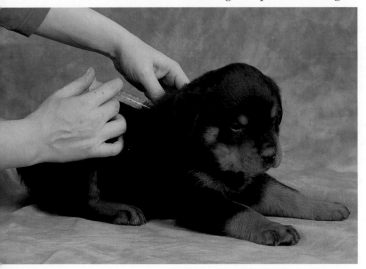

Vaccinations have saved the lives of thousands of dogs.

Leptospirosis

Leptospirosis is a bacterial disease transmitted primarily

The Vaccination Controversy

Vaccination procedures have been under fire for quite some time, with some researchers advocating a not-so-traditional approach. The majority of experts agree that vaccinations are an important part of canine preventive medicine. They are also in agreement when it comes to puppy vaccinations, and the need to continue vaccinating all dogs for rabies. However, modern medicine and technology have helped scientists and researchers become more knowledgeable about vaccines, and canine medicine in general. As a result, many vaccines have improved and so too has the duration of immunity. Therein lies the controversy regarding the necessity of continuing to vaccinate dogs on a yearly basis, and the long-term health risks associated with this practice. Some veterinarians advocate rotating yearly vaccines using a single component vaccine—a vaccine, for example, that contains parvovirus rather than combination vaccines that contain parvovirus, distemper, and hepatitis. A Rottweiler would, for instance, receive a vaccination for disease A one year, and a vaccination for disease B the following year. Other veterinarians recommend giving the vaccinations together, but only every three years.

Modern medicine and technology will help to keep your Rottweiler happy and healthy, but the controversy surrounding vaccinations is not likely to fade anytime too soon. No doubt, the future will bring many changes in traditional thinking as it pertains to vaccinations. Therefore, it is important to know the options and discuss vaccination protocol with your veterinarian.

through the urine of infected animals. The disease can get into water or soil and can survive for weeks to months. Rottweilers, as well as humans, can become infected through contact with the contaminated urine or the contaminated water or soil. A Rottweiler who drinks, swims, or walks through contaminated water also can become infected. Symptoms can include fever, vomiting, abdominal pain, diarrhea, loss of appetite, weakness, lethargy, stiffness, severe muscle pain, and even death. Treatment includes antibiotics, and in cases of kidney failure, dialysis.

Lyme Disease

Lyme disease was first diagnosed in 1975, in Lyme, Connecticut, yet there is evidence that it existed in wildlife for many years prior to that date. Lyme disease, a bacterial infection caused by a slender spiral microorganism identified as *Borrelia burgdorferi*, is transmitted to humans and dogs through the bite of an infected deer tick, also known as the black-legged tick. Cases of Lyme disease are most prevalent in the northeastern, mid-Atlantic, and north-central states. If infection occurs, the spirochetes migrate, invade, and penetrate into connective tissues, skin joints, and the nervous system. However, illness may not show up for months after initial exposure to an infected tick, and the severity of the disease may vary depending on the dog's age and immune status. The most common symptoms are a fever of between 103 and 105°F (39 and 40.5°C), shifting leg lameness, swelling in the joints, large lymph nodes, and lethargy. Treatment usually involves an oral antibiotic prescription, but the disease can be difficult to cure and the symptoms may reoccur. Occasionally, it develops into a chronic state—becoming a "waxing and waning" illness where the symptoms come and go. Vaccines are available, but their protection is not absolute.

Parvovirus

Parvo is a highly contagious gastrointestinal disease that normally affects puppies more frequently than adult dogs. Of particular interest to Rottweiler breeders and owners is the increased risk to Rottweilers. Unfortunately, experts do not yet understand the underlying biologic basis for the breed's predisposition to parvo.

The majority of puppies infected are under 6 months of age, with the most severe cases seen in puppies younger than 12 weeks of age. Some puppies have more immunity to the virus than others—especially if their mother was properly vaccinated, because she will transfer immunity to the virus in the colostrum, or first milk. These antibodies may be present in the puppy for up to 20 to 22 weeks, but may not be protective the entire time. Therefore, it is important to follow up with your puppy's regular puppy shots or vaccination schedule as recommended by your veterinarian.

The virus is spread through the stools of infected dogs and attacks rapidly dividing cells like those in the digestive track and cells in your puppy's bone marrow. The normal incubation period—the time period between exposure to the virus and the time when symptoms begin to appear—can be as short as 4 days after exposure. No drugs are available to kill the parvovirus once a dog is infected. The dog's own immunity has to rid itself of the virus. When dealing with parvovirus, time is of the essence, and it is critically important that you seek veterinary attention immediately if you suspect your puppy has been exposed to the parvovirus or your puppy shows any symptoms that can include vomiting, diarrhea (often dark and bloody), loss of appetite, lack of energy, fever, and dehydration. In very young puppies, parvovirus can also affect the heart muscle, which can lead to death within a matter of hours.

The virus is resistant to environmental influences, such as heat and cold, and can survive on clothes, dog bowls, and kennel floors for 5 months—or longer in the right conditions. It is important to discard all feces from an infected dog and disinfect areas with a 1:30 diluted solution of bleach and water. Equally important, throw away your puppy's food and water bowls, and either toss or bleach his bedding to prevent further spreading of the virus. And do not neglect your own hygiene. Be sure to thoroughly wash your hands, shoes, and clothing after handling infected materials.

Health Journal

Keep track of your dog's worming, flea, and vaccination schedule on a calendar or journal that you look at frequently. Write down the dates he was treated, and then flip ahead and jot down the dates he's due for another treatment. Not all veterinarians send reminders, and more than a few get lost in the mail.

Rabies

All warm-blooded animals—including humans—are at risk for contracting rabies. Rabies is a viral disease that affects the brain and is almost invariably fatal once symptoms begin to appear. Transmission of the virus is almost always through a bite from a rabid animal. The virus is relatively slow moving, with the average incubation time from exposure to brain involvement (in dogs) being between 2 weeks to 6 months.

Clinical symptoms vary within the different stages of rabies. If you suspect your Rottweiler has been bitten by a wild animal or infected dog or cat, it is always best to err on the side of caution and seek veterinary assistance immediately. No known cure for rabies exists. However, vaccination is the best way to prevent infection, and properly vaccinated animals are at a relatively low risk of contracting the disease.

HEALTH ISSUES IN THE ROTTWEILER

Like most breeds, the Rottweiler is not immune to health problems, and genetic diseases remain of paramount importance to reputable breeders. Certainly, the good health care you provide your Rottweiler will help to influence and prolong his life. But sometimes, regardless of your meticulous attention and best efforts, a Rottweiler, for whatever reason, will develop a health problem.

To a large degree, your Rottweiler's health is dictated by the genes he inherited from his ancestors, primarily his parents. He is the sum of his genetic makeup, which lays the foundation for his size, markings, structure, temperament, work ethic, and overall health.

The genetic problems of major concern to Rottweiler breeders

and owners include cataracts, cruciate ligament ruptures, hip and elbow dysplasia, panosteitis, bone cancer, subaortic stenosis, and hypothyroidism, among others.

Anterior Cruciate Ligament (ACL) Ruptures

No doubt you have heard of athletes who injure or "blow out" their knees. These types of injuries are usually a result of a specific trauma. Dogs, too, are susceptible to knee injuries, with one of the more common knee injuries being a ruptured anterior cruciate ligament. With dogs, however, many of the injuries are attributed less to a specific trauma and more to a gradual weakening or degeneration of the ligament.

A dog's stifle joint—also known as the knee joint—is formed by three bones: the femur (the long bone extending down from the hip), the tibia (the bone between the knee and ankle), and the patella (the kneecap). These bones come together to form the stifle joint, and are joined together by a number of muscles and ligaments. Unlike the hip and elbow joints that are designed to prevent excess or abnormal movement, a dog's knee joint has no interlocking bones. Instead, it must rely solely on the soft tissue structures in and around the joint to hold it in place and protect it from injury.

The anterior cruciate ligament and the posterior cruciate ligament crisscross, forming an X in the knee joint and keeping the femur and tibia from moving back and forth across each other. The ligament in the front is the anterior cruciate ligament. The one crossing behind is the posterior cruciate ligament. The anterior cruciate ligament provides the most stability to the knee during weight bearing and is the ligament that tends to rupture. When a partial or complete tear occurs, the knee's stability is severely weakened, which in turn causes inflammation and damage to the joint.

The cause of the tearing is generally unknown. Many experts believe that the excessive release of degradative enzymes in the tissue of the knee joint degrades the collagen within the ligament and weakens the ACL, predisposing it to rupture. A dog who twists on his hind leg, slips on a slippery surface, or makes a sudden or fast turn while running can rupture his cruciate ligament. Because of the nontraumatic nature of torn ACLs, a significant chance exists—some experts suggest between 30 and 80 percent—that the opposite ACL will also tear. Equally important, obesity puts additional weight on the knee, and overweight

Rottweilers tend to have more occurrences of ruptured ACLs than their lean counterparts.

Symptoms can occur suddenly or gradually and include stiffness or limping in the dog's hind leg, particularly after exercise or prolonged periods of rest. It is not uncommon for the limping to increase, becoming progressively worse over time. Some dogs will sit with their hind leg off to one side. Other dogs may have an intermittent clicking noise when walking.

As with other orthopedic problems, diagnosis usually involves a physical examination, manipulation of the joint, and observation of joint movement. A definitive diagnosis can be made with the help of X-rays. Surgery is generally the most common method of correction. The longer the knee goes untreated, the greater the chance of irreversible arthritic conditions developing.

Atopic Dermatitis (AD)

When a Rottweiler is allergic to a particular substance, his body reacts to certain molecules called allergens, which trigger an allergic reaction. Atopic dermatitis is an allergic skin condition caused by a hypersensitivity to environmental allergens that usually include house dust, dust mites, and molds. They can also include tree, grass, and weed pollens. These lightweight, airborne allergens move freely and easily through the air. Exposure triggers an immune system response that causes itchy, inflamed skin, which causes a dog to chew, scratch, and even bite at their skin.

AD usually occurs during the summer and fall seasons, when pollen activity is high. The age of onset is usually between 1 and 3 years of age. Diagnosis is based on clinical signs and a process of elimination, such as a skin scraping to rule out parasites. The treatment for AD is very similar to flea allergy dermatitis—reduce

Dog Facts

- A snoozing dog has a heart rate about the same as a resting human—about 80 beats per minute.
- A working dog's heart rate can reach 274 beats per minute—almost double the rate of a healthy, active human.
- Dogs have about 25 times more olfactory (smell) receptors than humans.
- A dog's supersensitive ears respond to lower volumes and higher pitches than humans. A human's hearing is best for sounds about 2,000 sound wave cycles per second—or about the same pitch as speech—and top out at about 20,000 cycles per minute. Dogs hear best at about 8,000 cycles per second, and can hear up to and slightly above 60,000 cycles per second.

exposure to the triggering allergens, hypoallergenic shampoos, topical anti-itch cream, and fatty acid supplements. A veterinarian may also prescribe antihistamines, corticosteroids or other medications for itching. .

Bloat

Gastric dilatation-volvulus (GDV), better known as bloat, is a life-threatening emergency that tends to occur in large-breed dogs with deep chests. It rarely occurs in small-breed dogs. Many breeds are susceptible to bloat, and it is considered a common cause of death in Rottweilers.

Dogs can die of bloat within several hours, and even with treatment, as many as 25 to 33 percent of dogs with GDV die. Therefore, every Rottweiler owner should understand the severity of the condition and be able to recognize the symptoms.

GDV is a two-part problem that involves the stomach expanding and then twisting. In the first part, a dog's stomach fills up with gas or fluids—or a combination of the two. If the gas or fluids can't escape, the stomach expands (gastric dilation). When the stomach expands, it puts pressure on the diaphragm and other organs, making it difficult for a dog to breathe. The expansion also compresses large veins in the dog's stomach, which in turn prevents blood from returning to the heart.

Good health care will help to prolong your Rottweiler's life.

When a dog's stomach is expanded, it can easily rotate on itself. Think about how an inflated balloon is easily twisted in the center, creating what looks like a sausage link. Once the stomach rotates, which is the "volvulus" part of the two-part GDV equation, the dog's stomach begins to die, and the dog's condition begins to deteriorate very rapidly.

Not all dogs who have a gas build-up or gastric dilatation develop the more serious volvulus or twisting of the stomach. However, almost all dogs who experience a twisting of the stomach develop it as a result of the stomach expanding.

Color-Blind Dogs?

Dogs do not see the same colors as humans do. Canine ophthalmologists believe dogs see the world similarly to a human who is red/green color-blind. Dogs should see a spectrum of what humans see as blues and yellows. No one can say for certain how dogs perceive the colors orange, red, and green. They may see them as grays or perhaps as blues and yellows. Dogs are, however, able to differentiate shades of gray that are indistinguishable to the human eye. So, before you begin thinking your Rottweiler is as blind as a bat—remember the red toy on the green grass might stand out like a sore thumb to you, but not to your dog.

Symptoms

The most obvious signs of GDV include a swollen or distended belly, abdominal pain, rapid and shallow breathing, retching or vomiting with nothing coming up, restlessness, and profuse salivation, which may indicate severe pain. If the stomach has twisted, the dog may go into shock and become pale, have a weak pulse, rapid heart rate, and he may collapse. If you suspect your dog has GDV, get him to a veterinarian immediately. Time is of the essence. Do not try to treat this problem at home.

Treatment consists of stabilizing the dog and then decompressing the stomach by passing a stomach tube or inserting a large needle into the stomach to release the gas or fluids. Once the dog has been stabilized, x-rays are taken to determine whether the stomach has twisted. If volvulus has occurred, surgery is performed to assess the health of the stomach and surrounding organs, reposition the stomach (if necessary), and suture the stomach in such a way as to prevent future twisting, which is also known as gastropexy. Without gastropexy, 75 to 80 percent of dogs will develop GDV again. If severe damage has occurred to the stomach or other organs, euthanasia may be the most humane option.

Prevention

Dogs who are susceptible to or have a tendency to develop GDV should be fed smaller meals several times throughout the day, as opposed to one large meal once a day. Rapid eating or gulping of food should be discouraged. Avoid any exercise for at least 2 hours after eating. The consumption of large amounts of water after any exercise should be avoided to limit stomach expansion.

Experts do not yet completely understand the causes of bloat.

However, understanding that GDV is a life-threatening emergency, recognizing the symptoms, and getting your dog to a veterinarian immediately will help to increase your dog's chance of survival.

Cataracts

Cataracts are not uncommon in dogs. In fact, they are one of the more common problems affecting the eyes of dogs, and a leading cause of vision loss in all dogs. A normal, healthy lens is transparent. The term cataract is used to define an abnormality of the lens in which opacity causes the passage of light to the retina to become obstructed. The opacity often resembles a cloudy film on the surface of the eye but, in fact, the opacity is deep inside a Rottweiler's eyeball.

Cataracts are classified by several factors including the age of onset (the age of the dog at the time the cataract develops) and the cause. Congenital cataracts are present at birth. Congenital is frequently confused with inherited. Inherited means the genes that are responsible for an inherited condition are present at birth. The inherited condition itself may be evident at birth, or may show up later in life. Most cataracts are inherited, but nonhereditary cataracts can also occur as a result of trauma or other diseases, such as diabetes.

The age at which a cataract develops is important for classifying the type of cataract and determining if it is a hereditary trait. A breeder who has her dogs' eyes examined yearly will have established a health record and know the age of the dog if and when cataracts began to develop. This provides valuable information to both the breeder and veterinarian. On the other hand, if a Rottweiler's eyes are not checked at 8 weeks of age or yearly thereafter, and the dog subsequently is diagnosed with cataracts at, say, 6 years old, it is more difficult to determine if they are genetic cataracts or some other form.

The most common cataracts in Rottweilers are juvenile cataracts. Juvenile simply refers to the age at which the cataract develops, which in the Rottweiler breed is generally prior to 2 years of age. These cataracts may progress to blindness, or they may remain small and not impair a Rottweiler's vision at all.

Cataracts also are classified by their location and the degree of opacity. Cataracts can assume a variety of appearances depending on the severity of the situation. They can appear as small white flecks in the eye, which may not cause any visual impairment. In more severe cases, where the opacity is nearly compete and the eye takes on a milky white hazy or cloudy appearance, vision loss may range from partial to complete blindness.

Your regular veterinarian may be able to confirm the presence of mature or complete cataracts, but small cataracts usually are found by first dilating the dog's pupil and then examining the lens with high-tech equipment found in veterinary ophthalmology clinics.

No medical treatment is available to prevent, reverse, or shrink cataracts. Surgery is the only known treatment, and new improved microsurgical techniques have increased the success rates of restoring vision to affected Rottweilers.

Unless cataracts are known to be specifically associated with a cause, such as trauma or damage to the eye, it is prudent to assume they are hereditary, and the dog should not be bred.

It is worth nothing that cataracts differ from nuclear sclerosis, which is a normal change that occurs in the lens of older dogs. It is the slight graying of the lens that owners frequently mistake for cataracts. It usually occurs in both eyes at the same time and occurs in most dogs over the age of 6 years.

Elbow Disease

Anatomically, a dog's elbow joint is similar to a human's elbow. It is a complicated hinge-type joint that is, in its simplest form, created by the junction of three different bones—the ulna, radius,

Your veterinarian can help you design an exercise program that is best suited for your dog.

and humerus. These bones fit and function together with little room for error, and all the parts must work harmoniously for maximum soundness and efficiency. Anything that alters the elbow configuration will affect a dog's ability to use his leg correctly.

Elbow disease—frequently referred to as elbow dysplasia—is really a syndrome for different elbow abnormalities that include ununited anconeal process (UAP), fragmented medial coronoid process (FCP), and osteochondritis desiccans (OCD).

- *Ununited anconeal process.* The anconeal process is a small, slightly hooked piece of bone on the upper end of the ulna that fits into a hole in the humerus and articulates, or moves, with the humerus. It starts out as cartilage and gradually turns to bone as it unites or fuses with the rest of the ulna. Generally, this takes place by the time the dog is about 5 months old. If the bone fails to fuse correctly to the rest of the ulna, an ununited anconeal process occurs. As a result, the humerus and ulna cannot interact correctly, leading to instability within the joint.

- *Fragmented medial coronoid process (FCP).* The coronoid process is a bone that moves with the ulna and humerus and also bears much of the weight of the dog. Like the anconeal process, the coronoid process starts out as cartilage and develops into bone as the puppy grows. If the bones fail to develop properly, too much weight is placed on the coronoid process, which can cause it to fracture or degenerate, exposing the underlying tissues of the bone. Generally this occurs very early in a dog's life—often before 6 months of age.

- *Osteochondritis desiccans (OCD).* In joints where different bones come together and move against each other, the surface of the bone is covered with cartilage, also known as articular cartilage, which acts as a cushion to protect the underlying bone from irritation or damage. In OCD, a portion of the cartilage cracks or breaks loose. This leads to degeneration within the joint, a very painful situation for a dog.

Symptoms of the three diseases are similar and can include lameness in the front legs that persists for more than a few days, reduction in range of movement, and pain when a veterinarian manipulates the joint. The next diagnostic step usually includes a set of high quality x-rays, and in some cases a computed tomography (CT) scan or exploratory surgery may be necessary to establish a definitive diagnosis. Depending on where you live, you may need to travel to a veterinary teaching hospital or specialized clinic.

Treatment varies depending on the diagnosis. With FCP and OCD, many experts first recommend medical treatment, which includes a specifically designed exercise program, dietary changes if weight reduction is necessary, and the use of nutraceuticals, such as glucosamine and chondroitin, as well as nonsteroidal anti-inflammatory medications. In some instances of FCP and OCD, surgery may be necessary. UAP generally is treated with surgery.

Entropion and Ectropion

Entropion is a condition in which the lower eyelid, along with the eyelashes, rolls into the eye, leading to possible damage and ulcerations of the cornea. One or both eyes may be involved and, in rare cases, the upper eyelid may also be affected. Symptoms include squinting, redness, and inflammation of the eye. Some dogs will scratch at the eye, possibly causing further damage. Surgery is the only treatment.

Ectropion is a condition in which the lower eyelid rolls outward, causing a looseness or drooping of the eyelid, which results in the exposure of an abnormally large amount of conjunctival lining. Resulting problems include chronic conjunctivitis and irritation to the cornea. Mild cases often are treated with eye drops or salves. Severe cases require surgery to remove excess tissue.

Hip Dysplasia

In simple terms, dysplasia means a developmental abnormality, which can include size, shape, or formation. Hip dysplasia is a defect in the conformation of the hip joint that can cause arthritis, resulting in weakness and lameness to a dog's rear quarters and severe debilitating pain. The resulting arthritis is frequently referred to as degenerative joint disease, arthrosis, or osteoarthritis.

While it is known to affect mostly giant- and large-breed dogs, hip dysplasia can occur in medium-sized breeds and even in small breeds, although rarely. It is important to breeders and owners because the Rottweiler is one of several breeds that appear to have a predisposition to hip dysplasia.

The Rottweiler is one of several breeds that appear to have a predisposition to hip dysplasia.

The hip is a ball-and-socket joint that forms the attachment of a Rottweiler's hind leg to his body. The ball portion of the joint is the head of the femur (the femoral head), while the socket portion or *acetabulum* is located on the pelvis. In a normal hip joint, the socket surrounds the ball, allowing the ball to rotate freely within the socket. To facilitate movement, the ball and socket are shaped to perfectly fit each other, and a ligament holds the ball and socket joint together. The area where the two bones actually touch each other is called the articular surface, which is smooth and cushioned with a layer of spongy cartilage. In a Rottweiler with normal hips, all these factors work together to result in maximum function, efficiency, and joint stability.

In a Rottweiler with hip dysplasia, an abnormal development of the hip joint results in excessive laxity or looseness. Over time, this looseness causes damage to the cartilage, which results in a lot of degradative enzymes being released into the joint. These enzymes decrease the synthesis of molecules that form an important joint protectant called proteoglycans. As a result, the cartilage begins to lose its thickness and elasticity, and that compromises the joints ability to handle the stress of day-to-day movement. As the erosion of the joint continues, the dog's body attempts to compensate, often producing secondary changes in the shapes of the bones composing the hip joint. Over time, the ligament can no longer hold the hip joint together and the articular surfaces of the two bones—the area where the ball and socket joint comes together— begin to lose contact with each other. When the two bones separate, it is called *subluxation*. Subluxation causes the problems associated with hip dysplasia and the resulting arthritis.

Symptoms

Symptoms of hip dysplasia vary, and it is difficult, if not impossible, to predict when or even if a dysplastic Rottweiler will show symptoms. Caloric intake, level of exercise, weather, and other environmental influences can affect the appearance of symptoms. Some dysplastic dogs with arthritis can still run,

Tips for Dogs with Hip or Elbow Dysplasia

Hip and elbow dysplasia are primarily inherited conditions, and no products on the market can prevent their development. However, several options may help to decrease the progression of degenerative joint disease while providing additional comfort to your pet.

- Weight management is the first and one of the most important things you can do for your Rottweiler's overall health. The extra pounds an overweight Rottweiler carries around put additional stress on his already compromised joints. An overweight Rottweiler is more susceptible to injuries. If necessary, seek veterinary assistance on the appropriate amount and type of food to feed.
- Exercise your dog regularly, but not to excess. Your veterinarian can help you design an exercise program that is best suited for your dog based on his overall health, weight, and joint condition. Exercise that provides good range of motion while limiting wear and tear on the joints, such as walking on surfaces with good traction or swimming, are usually recommended. Retrieving games where a dog is jumping, such as catching a ball or flying disc, are hard on his joints and can exacerbate joint problems.
- Whether your Rottweiler is young or old, he is sure to appreciate a warm and comfortable place for sleeping. Orthopedic beds are ideal, and provide the necessary cushioning for dogs with sore joints. Equally important, dogs with aches and pains will be able to get on and off an orthopedic bed much easier than other types of soft, fluffy beds. Be sure the bed is placed in a warm spot away from drafts.
- Like people, dogs love a good massage! Consider regular visits to a canine chiropractor or physical therapist. Or, ask an expert to show you how to massage your dog to help relax his muscles and promote a good range of motion in his joints. As with most activities relating to dogs, start slow. If your Rottweiler is in pain, you do not want to risk aggravating the situation.
- For dogs with moderate amounts of pain or lameness, consider building or purchasing a ramp so that your Rottweiler does not need to maneuver steps or stairs. In some cases, stairs or steps may be enough to prevent your dog from getting outside to urinate or defecate.

jump, play, and work, while other dogs show severe lameness.

That said, the symptoms associated with hip dysplasia are not unlike the symptoms associated with other causes of arthritis. Many Rottweilers walk or run with an altered gait and will frequently resist movements that require them to fully extend or flex their rear legs. Some Rottweilers may experience stiffness and pain in their rear legs after exercise or first thing in the morning when they get up and start to move about. Other dogs will run with a "bunny hopping" gait. Some dogs will limp, decrease their level of physical activity, and may need help getting up.

Diagnosis and Treatment

A veterinarian usually can give a preliminary diagnosis of hip dysplasia, which is made through a combination of a physical examination and x-rays. For a definitive evaluation, x-rays can be submitted to the Orthopedic Foundation for Animals (OFA), where three radiologists evaluate the hip joint and a consensus score is assigned. This is the traditional and most common method of evaluation.

Hips evaluated by the OFA are categorized and graded as:

- Normal (Excellent, Good, Fair)
- Borderline
- Dysplastic (Mild, Moderate, Severe)

A Rottweiler puppy can be x-rayed and receive a preliminary hip evaluation as young as 4 to 5 months of age. However, he cannot receive an OFA grade and certification until he is at least 2 years old. At that time, new x-rays must be submitted to the OFA for evaluation.

An alternative to OFA x-rays is a diagnostic method used by the University of Pennsylvania Hip Improvement Program (PennHIP), which uses distraction/compression radiographic views to obtain accurate and precise measurements of joint laxity—the primary cause of degenerative joint disease. This procedure is performed while the dog is heavily sedated, to provide the greatest amount of muscle relaxation, and involves using weights and an external device to help push the head of the femur (the ball portion of the ball-and-socket joint) into or away from the hip socket. The amount of joint looseness when the dog's hips are completely relaxed is given a distraction index (DI), which strongly correlates with the future development of degenerative joint disease.

The Rottweiler is one of several breeds that appear to have a predisposition to hip dysplasia.

Treatment of hip dysplasia varies and can include nutraceuticals, such as glucosamine, chondroitin, and methylsulfonylmethane (MSM), or over-the-counter drugs, such as buffered aspirin. Your veterinarian may also choose to prescribe a highly effective pain reliever. Depending on the age of your Rottweiler and the severity of the joint degeneration, your veterinarian may recommend surgery, which can include a femoral head ostectomy, triple pelvic osteotomy, or, in some cases, a total hip replacement.

Hypothyroidism

The thyroid gland, a butterfly shaped gland located near your Rottweiler's larynx

(Adam's apple), has a number of important functions, but is best known for its role in regulating metabolism. Hypothyroidism is the condition that occurs when not enough thyroid hormone is produced. The primary cause of hypothyroidism is thought to be the destruction of the thyroid gland. In about 50 percent of the cases, the destruction is thought to be caused by the dog's own immune system killing the cells of the thyroid gland. The other 50 percent is caused by atrophy of the thyroid tissue and the infiltration of the tissue by fat.

The thyroid hormone is critical in a dog's normal cellular metabolic function. A deficiency of the thyroid hormone affects the metabolic function of all organ systems. As a result, the symptoms vary and are nonspecific—no one particular symptom points toward a thyroid problem. Rather, when several symptoms, such as lethargy, hair loss, dry coat, excessive shedding, anemia, weight gain, exercise intolerance, and difficulty maintaining body temperature, are combined—it suggests to the veterinarian the possibility of hypothyroidism. However, the clinical symptoms of many diseases and conditions can mimic those of hypothyroidism. A blood test confirms or refutes the diagnosis. The good news is that hypothyroidism can be treated successfully with a daily dose of a synthetic thyroid hormone.

Careful breeders try to ensure that their Rottweilers are free from inherited disorders.

Osteosarcoma (Bone Cancer)

Osteosarcoma is an aggressive cancer of the bone that usually develops below the elbow or near the knee, and near the growth plates. In a high percentage of the cases, the cancer metastasizes to the lungs. It also can spread to the liver and kidneys, but rarely spreads to adjacent bones.

Osteosarcoma tends to affect older dogs, with the average age being around 7.5 years. However, an increased incidence of osteosarcomas has been observed in 1- and 2-year-old dogs. It is also more common in large or giant breeds and, unfortunately, the Rottweiler is one of those breeds affected.

The most common symptoms associated with osteosarcoma are lameness, swelling in the joint, and pain. Once the tumor has been positively identified as osteosarcoma through x-rays or, if necessary, a biopsy, the affected limb is usually amputated (although there is disagreement among experts as to whether or not amputation increases survival time). Additional treatments generally include chemotherapy and radiation. Aggressive treatments may improve survival in some dogs. However, only a small percentage of dogs—roughly 15 percent—diagnosed with osteosarcoma are cured. A large percentage of dogs are euthanized because of unmanageable pain or because of fractures in the affected and weakened bone structure.

Panosteitis (Pano)

Panosteitis, or pano, is a bone disease of dogs characterized by sudden and painful bouts of lameness. Rottweilers, as well as other large-breed dogs, are prone to the disease, which commonly lasts between 2 and 5 months, but can last for as long as 18 months.

A great deal of speculation has surrounded the cause of panosteitis but, unfortunately, experts do not know what causes the disease. Originally, it was suspected that a bacterial infection might be the culprit. Other theories included a possible viral connection or a link between modified live distemper vaccines and panosteitis. Others claim that nutrition, particularly protein and fat concentrations in a dog's diet, may have an impact on the incidence of panosteitis. One must also consider the potential genetic link or component because of the greatly increased incidence in certain breeds and families of dogs. It is important to note that none of these theories have been substantiated at this time.

Males are affected more commonly than females, and the disease cycle is more predictable and repeatable in males. Male Rottweilers tend to show symptoms somewhere between 6 and 18 months of age. A female usually has her first episode in association with her first heat cycle. Symptoms include a history of sudden lameness that generally lasts between 2 and 14 days. The lameness is not associated with any trauma or injury, and it is not unusual for the lameness to shift from leg to leg.

Diagnosis of the disease usually is based on a combination of clinical symptoms, such as shifting lameness, pain upon palpation of the bones, and often anorexia or lethargy. Several other diseases have similar symptoms, so x-rays are usually recommended to provide a more definitive diagnosis.

The most common therapeutic treatments are over-the-counter pain relievers, such as buffered aspirin or painkillers prescribed by your veterinarian. In severe cases, your veterinarian may prescribe a steroid but, because of the long-term side effects, painkillers are usually the first option. It is worth noting that drugs designed for humans should never be given to a dog without first seeking veterinary advice.

The good news is that panosteitis is self-limiting—meaning that, after it runs its course, very few long-term problems occur and the need for further treatment is unlikely. Because other diseases show similar symptoms, revisit your veterinarian if symptoms persist or your Rottweiler does not respond to treatment.

Hypothyroidism Facts

Hypothyroidism is most common in middle-aged dogs between 4 and 10 years of age. Additionally, it usually affects mid- to large-sized dogs, with some breeds (including Rottweilers) appearing to have a predisposition to the disease.

Subaortic Stenosis (SAS)

Aortic stenosis, also known as subvalvular aortic stenosis, is a narrowing just above or below the aortic valve that causes a partial obstruction of blood flow from the left ventricle of the heart, through the aortic valve, and into the aorta. If you remember high school biology, the left ventricle is the section of the heart that pumps oxygenated blood via the aortic valve into the aorta and then into the vital organs. The sub of subaortic stenosis identifies the defect—or constriction—as being located just below the aortic valve. It is the most common form of aortic stenosis.

The narrowing (stenosis) is caused by the abnormal formation of nodules, or a fibrous ridge or ring of tissue, which causes a partial obstruction of blood flow. Think of SAS in terms of water running through a garden hose. If you were to put your thumb over part of the end of the hose, the water speed increases, producing a more powerful spray and a hissing noise, which is caused by the same volume of water trying to get through the restricted opening. In an SAS-affected dog, the heart must work harder to compensate for the partial blockage and to pump the same volume of blood through the narrowed opening and into the dog's vital organs. As a result, the dog's heart develops more muscles to push harder, which can lead to an irregular heartbeat, lack of blood to the heart, congestive heart failure, or sudden death.

An SAS-affected dog carries SAS genes, and the disease generally develops over the first year of life. In mild cases, the disease may not affect the quality or longevity of the dog's life. In severe cases, affected dogs usually die at a young age. Symptoms can include exercise intolerance, fainting, and even sudden death. However, not all sudden deaths in Rottweilers can or should be automatically attributed to SAS.

Diagnosis and Treatment

Diagnosing SAS is a bit of an art. A veterinarian—even a very skilled veterinarian—can easily miss subtle or even moderate murmurs. Therefore, diagnosis begins with a canine cardiologist listening for a heart murmur, which is an abnormal sound detected when the heart beats. It is a signal that something has changed in the normal blood flow, but it does not necessarily mean the change will significantly affect your Rottweiler's health. In an affected puppy, enough of a heart murmur exists at 8 to 10 weeks of age to be detected by a cardiologist. If a murmur is detected, the cardiologist will perform additional tests including an echocardiogram, which measures blood flow, to confirm or refute the diagnosis. If, on the other hand, no murmur is found, it is unlikely the dog will develop SAS. The dog should be rechecked at 12 months of age and, if he is found to free of murmurs, he can receive a cardiac clearance from the Orthopedic Foundation of America.

Rottweilers diagnosed with SAS should avoid strenuous exercise, especially in hot weather. Equally important, the dog should not be allowed to become overweight because this puts additional strain on an already compromised heart. A veterinarian also may prescribe medications to improve exercise tolerance, reduce the heart's workload, and prevent abnormal heart rhythms. In some cases, surgery may be recommended.

DEALING WITH PARASITES

Parasites. They sound grotesque and, to the average dog owner, they are. Unfortunately, it is highly likely that, sometime within your Rottweiler's life, he will suffer from an internal parasite (like worms) or an external one (like fleas). Both types need treatment. Left unchecked, parasites can cause debilitating and life-threatening problems.

External Parasites

Demodectic Mange

Would you be surprised to learn your Rottweiler has mites? Not just a case of mites, but mites that spend their entire lives in his hair follicles and skin glands? Demodectic mange is a skin disease caused by a tiny mite called *Demodex canis.* In small numbers, these mites are typically present on your dog's skin and, in most cases, usually cause no problems.

The development of demodicosis is complex and not completely understood, but here's what experts do know: The mites are passed from a mother to a puppy in the first week or so of life. Demodectic mange is not an inherited condition, but there appears to be a correlation between a puppy's ineffective or sensitive immune system, which may have a genetic component, and the mange itself. Two forms of the disease exist: localized and generalized. Localized is the most common and occurs in dogs usually under 1 year of age. Lesions usually are associated with some hair loss, because the mites prefer to live in the hair follicles. Lesions can appear as crusty, red skin, and can occasionally a have a greasy or moist appearance. Most of these lesions are confined to the muzzle, eyes, and other areas around the head and usually clear up as the puppy grows and develops his own immunity.

Generalized demodicosis is a more severe version characterized by lesions and areas of hair loss over the entire body, including the head, neck, stomach, legs, and feet, with lesions commonly aggravated by secondary bacterial infections. In severe cases, dogs can become quiet ill, developing lethargy, fever, and loss of appetite.

Demodectic mange is identified by clinical diagnosis of lesions and skin scrapings to confirm the presence of mites. All dogs have mites, so the visual identification of lesions is an equally important part of the diagnosis. Treatment for localized cases usually involves

**Early Detection
is Key**

Subaortic stenosis is a potentially deadly condition that is difficult to diagnose. A puppy found to have a heart murmur at 8 weeks of age should be retested at 1 year to make sure he is not likely to develop SAS.

shampoos, dips, and topical ointments or creams. Generalized cases require a more aggressive approach including dips, anti-parasitic drugs, and antibiotics to treat inflamed and infected lesions.

Fleas

If you own a Rottweiler, you no doubt know a thing or two about fleas! One bite from these pesky creatures can cause itching for days. And where one flea exists, it is a safe bet that plenty more are lurking in your carpet, furniture, bedding, and on your precious Rottweiler! What you may not know is there are over 2,200 species of fleas worldwide.

In North America, only a few species of fleas commonly infest dogs. The *Ctenocephalides felis,* also known as the domestic cat flea, likes both cats and dogs, and is the most common flea responsible for wreaking havoc with your Rottweiler. They are about 1/8-inch (.3 cm) long, slightly smaller than a sesame seed, and generally brown or black in color. These wingless bloodsuckers are responsible for spreading tapeworms to dogs and causing serious allergy dermatitis. In serious infestations, fleas can cause anemia, especially in puppies.

Eradicating fleas is easier said than done. Pupae can remain dormant in the cocoon for up to 6 months, which is important to remember when planning flea control. If you live where the temperature freezes, count your blessings. The cat flea is susceptible to cold, and no life stage of the flea can survive when exposed to temperatures below roughly 37°F (3°C).

To control and eliminate fleas, try these steps:

- *Clean everything your dog has come in contact with.* Wash his dog beds and blankets and mop up floors. Vacuum all carpets, rugs, and furniture. Immediately dispose of vacuum bags, because eggs can hatch in them.
- If necessary, remove the dense vegetation near your home, dog yard, or kennel area—these spaces offer a damp microenvironment that is favorable to flea development.
- Treat your Rottweiler and any other household pets that can serve as hosts, such as other dogs, cats, and ferrets.
- A number of insecticides and insect growth regulators are available for use in the home and have proven effective. However, it is worth noting that some insecticides are toxic: read all labels and follow directions carefully.

- A number of on-animal flea control products are available, such as shampoos, sprays, dips, powders, and flea collars. Many of these products have been around for years, but remember that many commercial and natural products may be toxic. They may irritate your Rottweiler's skin or cause health problems.
- The advent of once-a-month squeeze-on oil products has made flea control much easier and more effective. Your veterinarian can assist you in choosing the right flea control products for your four-legged friend.

Ticks

Unlike fleas, which are insects and have six legs, ticks, like mites and spiders, have eight legs. There are approximately 850 species of these blood-sucking parasites that burrow into your Rottweiler's skin and engorge themselves with blood, expanding to many times their size. They are dangerous because they can secrete a paralysis-causing toxin and can spread serious diseases such as Lyme disease, Rocky Mountain spotted fever, Texas fever, tularemia, babesiosis, and canine ehrlichiosis. It is not unusual for a tick to be infected with and transmit more than one disease. Therefore, it is not at all uncommon to see a dog infected with more than one disease at a time. In severe infestations, anemia and even death may occur.

Your Rottweiler is most likely to pick up ticks in wooded or grassy areas and overgrown fields. Ticks commonly embed themselves between the toes, in the ears, and around the neck but can be found elsewhere on the body. Each species has its own favored feeding sites on your Rottweiler.

Controlling ticks on your Rottweiler is not unlike the process for flea control. You must be committed and diligent. Treat your yard, house, doghouse, dog blankets, and your dog with a product specifically designed for ticks. A number of over-the-counter products are available such as sprays, foggers, powders, dips, shampoos, and collars. Unlike fleas, ticks are not susceptible to cold weather, so you will need to treat your yard late into the fall and early winter. Again, many of these products may be toxic. It is important to read all labels and follow directions

Flea Control Tip

Flea-control products are most effective when used in conjunction with a rigorous flea control program. A flea collar alone will not provide your Rottweiler with a flea-free environment.

carefully. When in doubt, consult your veterinarian before purchasing and using any tick control products.

Avoiding tick-infested areas during the peak tick season helps. When taking your Rottweiler for a walk, do not allow him to wander off designated paths or near low, overhanging branches and shrubs where ticks are likely to be waiting for an unsuspecting Rottweiler to pass by. Your local university or health department should be able to provide you with information on the types of ticks found in your area and their peak seasons.

How to Safely Remove a Tick

Removing an attached tick is not terribly difficult, once you get past any queasiness about doing so.

- Always use a pair of tweezers or a specially designed tick-removing tool. Small curved hemostats or curved-tip jeweler tweezers also work well.
- Grasp the tick as close as possible to where it enters your dog's skin.
- Pull slowly, firmly, and steadily in an outward direction. Don't jerk, squeeze, or twist the tick.
- After removing the tick, place it in a jar of alcohol to kill it. Some experts recommend keeping the tick alive in a sealed, dated vial for at least 1 month in case symptoms of tick-borne diseases develop. You can discuss this option with your veterinarian.
- It is not unusual for a small welt or skin reaction to occur once a tick is removed. Clean the bite wound with a disinfectant. If you want, apply an antibiotic ointment.

If you simply cannot bring yourself to remove a tick, take the dog to your veterinarian. Ticks must be removed, and the sooner the better.

Internal Parasites

Internal parasites are called endoparasites, meaning they live inside your Rottweiler's body. The most common are roundworms, hookworms, tapeworms, and whipworms. A number of deworming medications are available at local pet stores and retail outlets. However, dewormers differ drastically in their safety and effectiveness in expelling worms form the body. Therefore, the wise choice is to have a veterinarian diagnose the specific type of internal parasite and then prescribe the proper deworming medication.

Flea Allergy Dermatitis

If your Rottweiler is sensitive to fleas, one bite from this tiny, nearly invisible pest can make his life (and yours!) miserable and plunge him into a vicious cycle of biting, scratching, and licking. Flea allergy dermatitis, also known as bite hypersensitivity, tends to be most prevalent during the summer when fleas are most rampant and annoying.

Fleas feeding on your Rottweiler inject saliva that contains different antigens and histamine-like substances, resulting in irritation and itching that can range from mild to downright nasty. Dogs with flea allergies may itch over their entire bodies, experience generalized hair loss, and develop red, inflamed skin and hot spots. They are frequently restless and uncomfortable, and may spend a great deal of time scratching, digging, licking, and chewing their skin.

Treatments vary and can be multifaceted. Of primary importance is a strict flea-control program to prevent additional infestation. Veterinarians frequently recommend hypoallergenic or colloidal oatmeal-type shampoos to remove allergens and topical anti-itch creams to soothe the skin. These products usually provide immediate, short-term relief, but are not a long-term solution. Additionally, fatty acid supplements, such as the omega-3 and omega-6 found in flaxseed and fish oils, are proving helpful in reducing the amount and effects of histamine. In some cases, veterinarians may prescribe corticosteroids or other medications to reduce itching.

Heartworms

Heartworms are potentially the most dangerous internal parasite and are found throughout the United States. Mosquitoes transmit the disease when they suck blood from an infected dog and then bite a healthy dog, thereby depositing larvae. The larvae grow inside the healthy dog, migrating through the dog's tissues, into the bloodstream, and eventually into the dog's heart. The larvae grow into adult worms between 6 and 14 inches (15.2 and 35.6 cm) in length. The process is relatively slow and can take about 6 to 7 months from the time the dog is bitten until an adult heartworm develops. A severely infected dog can have several hundred heartworms in his heart and vessels. The worms can completely fill and obstruct the heart chambers and the various large blood vessels leading from the heart to the lungs.

Dogs with heartworm infections may not show symptoms until the damage is extensive and the disease is well advanced. A chronic cough is often the first symptom followed by a decrease in appetite, loss of weight, listlessness, and fatigue after light exercise. Some dogs accumulate fluid in their abdomens and take on the pot-bellied appearance. In rare situations, the dog may die of sudden heart failure.

Diagnosis is usually done with a blood test that detects the presence of adult antigens in the blood. Heartworm treatment is not without risk because some—but not all—of the drugs used to kill the adult worms contain arsenic. The death of the worms also can create blood clots in a dog, which also presents life-

threatening problems. The protocol your veterinarian chooses depends on the severity of infection and whether your Rottweiler's kidney and liver functions can tolerate the treatment.

Preventive medications are available and are highly recommended, but must never be given to a dog who is already infected with adult worms. It is imperative that you consult with your veterinarian before starting any preventive treatment for heartworms.

Hookworms

Hookworms are another common pet invader—especially in puppies. They are only about 1/2-inch (1.3 cm) long, but they can cause serious health problems for your Rottweiler, including diarrhea, vomiting, and life-threatening anemia. A Rottweiler's gums may appear pale, the dog may be weak, and sometimes black, tarry stools can be seen. In severe cases, a blood transfusion may be necessary.

The adult hookworms have teeth-like structures or hooks that attach to the lining of your Rottweiler's intestine and feed on his oxygen-carrying blood. Adult hookworms then lay eggs that are passed in the dog's feces, where they hatch into larvae. Thus the cycle of infestation continues.

A Rottweiler can become infected when larvae enter through the skin and migrate through the bloodstream to the lungs and trachea. The larvae are then coughed up and swallowed, where they attach themselves to the intestinal wall.

Ingesting contaminated food or water, licking his contaminated feet, or ingesting an infected host can also infect a Rottweiler. Most ingested larvae pass directly down to the intestine, where they mature into adults.

A puppy can become infected when larvae migrate to the uterus or mammary glands of a pregnant bitch, thereby infecting the fetuses or nursing puppies.

Hookworms are contracted either through a dog's mother or through contaminated soil and feces, which makes sanitary practices paramount. All fecal material should be removed daily. When walking in public places, do not allow your dog to come in contact with other dogs' feces.

Roundworms

Roundworms, often called ascarids, are one of the most common parasites of the canine digestive tract. They live in the small intestine of your Rottweiler and are usually 3 to 4 inches (7.62 to 10.2 cm) long, but can be up to 7 inches (17.8 cm) long. They tend to look quite a bit like spaghetti.

Most puppies are born with roundworms, despite a breeder's exceptional sanitary whelping conditions, and most puppies require deworming at an early age. A pregnant bitch who has roundworms can pass them to her puppies in two ways. The dormant larvae in her tissues can migrate through the uterus and placenta and into the lungs of the unborn puppy. When the puppy is born, he coughs up the larvae, swallows them, and they mature in his intestines. Puppies also can become infected through ingestion of their mother's milk.

Dogs also can ingest roundworms when they eat an infected animal, such as a rodent, or when they ingest soil contaminated with roundworm eggs. Rottweilers who like to snack from the cat's litter box can pick up a roundworm infection by eating feces containing roundworm eggs.

Roundworms can cause serious problems for dogs and huge headaches for owners. When they infect your Rottweiler's intestines, they absorb nutrients, interfere with digestion, and can damage the lining of the intestine. In more severe infestations, dogs may be thin

Check your Rottweiler for ticks and fleas after he's been outside.

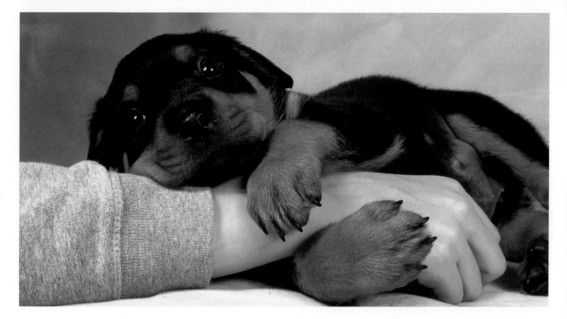

Most puppies are born with roundworms, and must be treated for the parasite at an early age.

and have a potbellied appearance. Their coats may be dry, dull, and rough looking. Some puppies may have intestinal discomfort and may cry as a result. Diarrhea or constipation and vomiting are also frequent symptoms. In some cases, a cough may develop due to the migration of the larvae through the respiratory system.

Roundworms are resistant to environmental conditions and most common disinfectants. They can adhere to hair, skin, and paws, so good hygiene and strict sanitation are important to minimize further contamination. Pick up feces on a daily basis. Once roundworms get into your soil, they can live for months or years. Tilling the soil to a depth of 8 to 12 inches (20.3 to 30.5 cm), removing it and replacing it with new soil, or paving the entire area is about the only way to totally solve the problem.

Tapeworms

Tapeworms are another common internal parasite found in dogs. While generally not life-threatening, they are definitely a problem. Unlike the whipworms, roundworms, and hookworms, tapeworms must go through an intermediate host in order for larvae to develop. In dogs, the most common hosts are fleas and lice, which ingest the eggs and subsequently set up housekeeping for the larvae.

When your Rottweiler ingests the flea or lice, it ingests the resident tapeworm. In certain species of tapeworms, rabbits and livestock can be the intermediate hosts. While less common, infections can occur when dogs eat or scavenge the internal body parts of wild game, the discarded parts of butchered livestock, or are given raw meat.

Tapeworms are flat and can be several feet long. They are segmented and consist of a head, neck, and then a number of segments, which contain large numbers of eggs that break away from the rest of the worm and are passed in the feces. The head usually has suckers or muscular grooves that enable the tapeworm to attach itself to your Rottweiler's intestine.

Tapeworms generally do not cause any symptoms, although diarrhea may be present. In severe infestations, your Rottweiler may exhibit abdominal discomfort or nervousness. The dog may vomit and in some cases experience convulsions, which are thought to be caused from the toxins produced by the tapeworm. The tiny segments, which look like tiny grains of uncooked rice, are passed through the feces. They are sometimes visible on the dog's rectum or in his stools. Some dogs will scoot their rear ends along the ground.

Getting rid of tapeworms can be difficult, because you must successfully eliminate the head of the tapeworm, otherwise it will regrow a new body. Flea and lice control are essential, otherwise your Rottweiler will continue to reinfest himself.

Whipworms

Whipworms get their name from the whiplike shape of the adult worm. Dogs become infected when they ingest food or water contaminated with whipworm eggs. The eggs are swallowed, hatch in the large intestine and, in about 3 months, the larvae mature into adults that attach to the intestinal lining and burrow their mouths into the intestinal wall, where they feed on blood. Adult worms lay eggs that are passed in the feces.

The symptoms vary depending on the number of worms in a dog's stomach. Mild infestations often produce no obvious symptoms in healthy individuals. Larger infestations, however, have more pronounced symptoms and can result in inflammation of the intestinal wall. Anemia is possible if hemorrhaging into the intestine occurs. Some dogs may experience diarrhea, mucus and blood in the stools, and loss of weight.

Whipworms can live in moist soil for years and are resistant to freezing. However, dry conditions, good drainage, sunlight, and

Tips when Removing a Tick

- Avoid using your fingers to remove ticks.
- Never handle ticks with your bare hands—it's a good idea to wear gloves.
- Do not use a hot match to get the tick to back out. It doesn't work.
- Do not try to smoother the tick with petroleum jelly or kill it by pouring rubbing alcohol on it. These old wives tales don't work.
- Do not flush ticks down the toilet. It doesn't kill them.

aeration of kennels, dog runs, and exercise areas will destroy whipworm eggs. Like roundworms, soil contamination is an enormous problem. To help reduce or prevent contamination, fecal matter should be picked up daily and kennel or dog run areas cleaned thoroughly, and if possible, be allowed to dry in direct sunlight.

Protozoal Intestinal Infections

Protozoa are one-celled organisms or parasites that infect the intestinal tract of dogs. Two of the most common protozoal infections that affect Rottweilers are coccidiosis and giardiasis.

Coccidia

Coccidia are a group of protozoan parasites that invade the cells of the small intestine, where they multiply rapidly and destroy tissue. Coccidia are spread in the feces of carrier animals. Once infected, the disease is referred to as coccidiosis. They are most common in puppies less than 6 months of age and in adult dogs with suppressed immune systems. They are also found in dogs who are under physiological stress, such as change of ownership, shipping, weaning, overcrowding, fatigue, dietary changes, or when other diseases are present.

As puppies age, they tend to develop a natural immunity to the effects of coccidia. An adult dog may carry coccidia in his intestines and shed the parasites in his feces, yet show no symptoms or experience any ill effects. A young Rottweiler may experience diarrhea streaked with blood, weight loss, diminished appetite, and, in some instances, even death.

Puppies are not born with the organisms in their body, but they may be exposed to the feces of their mother or to the environment. If she is shedding the infective parasites in her feces, then the young puppies will likely ingest them, and coccidia will develop in their intestines. This is by far the most common mode of infection in young dogs. However, puppies can be infected or reinfected when they groom themselves or their siblings. Cockroaches and flies can also carry coccidia from one location to another, and a Rottweiler who eats mice or other animals infected with coccidia can also become infected.

Coccidiosis is highly contagious, and any infected puppy is contagious to other puppies. Therefore, to control the spread of coccidiosis, practice strict sanitary practices. Fecal matter should be removed daily, and water and food should be housed so that it cannot become contaminated with feces. These practices reduce the potential for infection, but do not guarantee that infections will not occur. Fortunately, coccidiosis is treatable with prescription drugs. The drugs do not kill the organisms but instead inhibit their reproductive capabilities.

Giardia

Giardia (pronounced GEE-are-DEE-uh) live in the small intestine of dogs. Infection with Giardia is called giardiasis. The microscopic parasites reproduce by dividing in two and then, after an unknown number of divisions, pass in the stool. Giardiasis has been nicknamed the backpackers' disease because it is commonly acquired by drinking infected water in high mountain lakes and streams. Beavers are most often blamed for contaminating the water by passing the intestinal organism in their feces. However, Giardia also can be tracked into your house or kennel on your shoes or boots.

Giardia prevents proper absorption of nutrients, damages the intestinal lining, and interferes with digestion. In many cases involving adult dogs, few symptoms are associated with giardiasis. Younger dogs may develop diarrhea or abnormal, soft or light-colored stools that have a bad odor and greasy appearance. Some dogs will not lose their appetite, but they may lose weight.

Thanks to the marvels of modern technology, new tests make Giardiasis easier to diagnose and allow veterinarians to begin treating the problem much earlier. Veterinarians differ in their treatment, because currently no drugs are approved for treating giardiasis in dog. Often, treatment is given to control secondary infection.

FIRST AID

Dogs have the uncanny ability to get into anything and everything—usually at the most inopportune and unexpected times and when you are miles from a veterinarian! Many minor situations, such as scrapes, nicks, abrasions, or a bout of diarrhea, can be successfully treated at home. However, in the event of more serious situations, it is imperative that you remain calm, act quickly and effectively, and be able to recognize urgent and life-threatening situations that require immediate veterinary attention including:

- Convulsions
- Electrocution (i.e., puppies chewing on electrical cords)
- Loss of consciousness
- Sudden paralysis
- Poisoning
- Traumatic injury (i.e., car accident, kicked by a horse)
- Choking
- Repeated or continuous vomiting and/or diarrhea that lasts for more than 24 hours
- Shock (rapid pulse and breathing, lowered body temperature, or lack of normal response)
- Labored breathing
- Bloated abdomen
- Disorientation, confusion

Prevention is always the best route. That said, in spite of your best intentions, accidents do happen. Therefore, familiarize yourself with the various emergency response protocols. A number of canine first aid books and videos are available through retail outlets and online. If possible, attend a canine first aid seminar and have a canine first aid kit on hand. You can purchase preassembled kits or assemble your own. Equally important, post in a conspicuous spot the following numbers:

- ASPCA Poison Control Hotline 1-888-426-4435 (a fee is charged to your credit card)
- Your veterinarian's number
- A 24-hour emergency veterinary clinic (in the event your vet's office is closed)
- The local animal control office, in case your dog is lost

When calling the Poison Control Hotline, provide information on the type of poison ingested, the amount, and the duration since ingestion, and any symptoms your dog is experiencing. Also give your Rottweiler's age, sex, and weight.

What's in a First Aid Kit?

First aid kits can vary in their content. Some specialty kits are designed for sporting dogs and contain enough

Alternative Medicine

Alternative medicine is a term used to broadly describe those methods and practices of medicine used in place of or in addition to conventional medical treatments. Traditional medicine is rooted in science, physics, chemistry, and biology, and its practices are backed by scientific data. While some alternative medicine has been around for thousands of years, it is empirical, meaning the evidence comes less from clinical trials and more from the anecdotes and testimonials of veterinarians and dog owners. As the demand for alternative medicine for humans has grown, so too has the demand for alternative veterinary medicine, which is sometimes referred to as Complementary and Alternative Veterinary Medicine (CAVM).

Alternative medicine encompasses a broad range of treatments including:
- Acupuncture
- Chiropractic
- Massage
- Herb, Natural Supplements, and Vitamin and Mineral Supplementation
- Homeopathy

The American Veterinary Medical Association has established guidelines for veterinary acupuncture, chiropractic, homeopathic, and holistic medicine. "Alternative" and "herbal" do not mean harmless; The Food and Drug Administration (FDA) does not regulate herbs and natural supplements, and these preparations can cause side effects or result in cross-reactions if combined with other supplements or medications. To prevent problems, always consult your veterinarian.

medical paraphernalia to perform minor surgeries, mini first aid kits clip on your belt for walks in the park or hiking, and home kits contain basic first aid equipment. Whether you choose to purchase a super colossal preassembled kit, a basic home kit, or customize your own, it should contain basic necessities including:

- Activated charcoal (available from pharmacists; it binds or neutralizes certain poisons)
- Alcohol or alcohol prep pads (for sterilizing scissors, tweezers; not for use on wounds)
- Aspirin (not nonsteroidal anti-inflammatory drugs, such acetaminophen or ibuprofen)
- Eye wash or saline solution (for flushing out eye contaminants)
- Eye ointment
- Gauze rolls and gauze pads
- Gloves (latex for protecting hands, prevent contamination of wounds)
- Hydrogen peroxide 3% USP
- Instant cold pack
- Instant heat wrap
- Iodine (for cleaning wounds)
- Ipecac (to induce vomiting, if necessary)

- Muzzle (a dog may try to bite if he is injured or scared)
- Ointments (triple antibiotic ointment inhibits bacterial growth in cuts, abrasions)
- Pill gun (for administering pills)
- Rehydrating solutions (to replace lost electrolytes)
- Scissors (to clip hair around wounds, cut gauze, etc.)
- Styptic pencil (stops bleeding if a nail is broken, torn, clipped too short)
- Thermometer (preferably digital)
- Tick-removal tool
- Turkey baster, bulb syringe, or large medical syringe (for flushing wounds)
- Tweezers
- Wraps (self-clinging, flexible elastic-type bandages for wrapping injuries)

EMERGENCIES

Be aware of what plants may be toxic to your Rottweiler.

Hopefully, you'll never have to deal with anything more serious than bumps and bruises. However, it is in your Rottweiler's best interest for you to be prepared for certain emergencies you may end up facing.

Choking

Dogs can choke on any number of items, from disemboweled doll parts to buttons to safety pins to dog bones. Stories have been told of slick, slimy tennis balls sliding down a Rottweiler's throat, becoming lodged and creating a life-threatening situation. Some Rottweilers choke on their food if they "wolf" it down too quickly. Any obstruction of your dog's airway is a life-threatening medical emergency and must be dealt with immediately to prevent brain damage or death.

The symptoms of choking vary; however, the most common signs include a coughing, gagging, or retching noise, and pawing at the side of the face. His tongue may turn blue, and he may collapse. If you suspect your dog is choking, do not wait until the dog collapses to get help.

If possible, pull your Rottweiler's lower jaw open and tilt his head upward. If an object is visible, try to remove it with your finger without pushing it deeper. It goes without saying that you should use extreme caution to avoid being bitten. Regardless of how friendly your dog might be, a panicked, choking dog is likely to bite as a reflex mechanism.

If the object cannot be removed easily, a Heimlich-type maneuver can be performed on dogs. Become familiar with the procedure before a medical emergency arises. Your veterinarian can show you how to perform the procedure.

For an adult or large dog: Hold your dog from behind, wrap your arms around his body just behind the ribs. Wrap one hand around the other to make a double fist, placing the double fist on his abdomen below the rib cage. Squeeze sharply a few times, quickly pressing upward and forward until the object is expelled or dislodged.

For puppies: Follow the above procedure, but rather than use a double fist, place the index and middle fingers of both hands on the puppy's abdomen below the rib cage. Press into the abdomen with a quick, upward thrust. It may take several tries to dislodge or expel the object.

Once you have cleared your dog's airway, have him examined by a veterinarian as soon as possible.

Heat

Heatstroke, also known as hyperthermia, is a life-threatening condition, and overweight Rottweilers, puppies, and older Rottweilers are more vulnerable to heat-induced illnesses than Rottweilers in good physical condition and otherwise excellent health.

The average body temperature of a dog is 101.5°F (38.6°C), with a normal range between 100°F and 102°F (37°C and 39°C). These core temperatures are based on rectal thermometer readings. While temperatures can vary throughout a dog's body, the core temperature is one of a number of mechanisms that maintain a constant internal

A Real Life Saver

Have your veterinarian show you the dog equivalent of the Heimlich maneuver—it could save your pet's life in an emergency.

condition (homeostasis); these mechanisms include blood pressure and blood chemistry. Heat-induced illnesses occur when a dog's normal body mechanisms cannot keep his temperature within a safe range.

Unlike humans, dogs do not sweat. Their primary cooling mechanisms are panting and conduction. When overheated dogs pant, they breathe in and out through their mouths. They inhale cool air and, as the air moves into their lungs, it absorbs heat and moisture. When they exhale, the hot air passes over their wet tongues and evaporation occurs, enhancing and maximizing heat loss and cooling their bodies.

Conduction, the second method of cooling, occurs when a dog lies down on a cool surface, such as a tile floor, grass, or wet concrete. The heat is transferred to the cool surface.

Four types of heat-induced illnesses can occur: heat cramps, heat exhaustion, heat prostration, and heatstroke. Heat cramps are muscle cramps caused by the loss of salt from a dog's system and by extreme exertion in hot weather. Heat cramps do not normally occur in dogs, and it is highly unlikely you will encounter them in a Rottweiler.

Heat Exhaustion

Heat exhaustion is the least severe of the heat-related illnesses, but it must taken seriously. It is often referred to as a mild case of heatstroke and is characterized by lethargy and an inability to perform normal activities or work, such as obedience, agility, or tracking because of extreme heat.

Heat Prostration

On the continuum of heat-induced illnesses, heat prostration is the next level. This is a moderate case of heatstroke, with a dog's core body temperature at around 104°F to 106°F (40° to 41.1°C) degrees. Possible signs include rapid panting, red or pale gums, weakness, vomiting, mental confusion, and dizziness. Do not delay in seeking immediate veterinary attention. Dogs with a moderate case of heatstroke can often recover without complicating health problems.

Heatstroke

Heatstroke is a severe form of heat prostration and occurs when a dog's body temperatures is over 106°F (41°C). Dogs

Toxic Substances

If yours is like most homes, it is undoubtedly a toxic hot-spot filled with items that can inadvertently harm your dog. A sampling of a few of the most common toxic threats include:

- Antifreeze (ethylene-glycol—a sweet-tasting liquid that is particularly attractive to dogs).
- Alcoholic drinks / liquor
- Batteries (i.e., for remote controls, cameras, toys—contain harsh chemicals that can cause severe damage to his mouth, stomach, and other internal organs)
- Chocolate (contains two deadly toxins: theobromine and caffeine)
- Fertilizers
- Garbage (rotting garbage is a concentrated source of bacteria, some of which produce dangerous toxins)
- Herbicides (weed killers, etc)
- Ice-melting or deicing salts.
- Insecticides (snail and rat baits, etc)
- Lead (surfaces painted with lead-based paint—chairs, tables, walls, plumbing materials, fishing weights and lures)
- Medications (anti-inflammatories, acetaminophen, cold and flu medications, vitamin supplements, antidepressants, etc.)
- Mothballs
- Plants—both indoor and outdoor

suffering from heatstroke display signs that include rapid panting, collapsing, inability to stand up, red or pale gums, thick and sticky saliva, weakness, vomiting (with or without blood), diarrhea, shock, fainting, or coma. This is a life-threatening medical emergency that can result in multiple organ system dysfunction involving the respiratory, cardiovascular, gastrointestinal, renal, and central nervous systems. Immediate veterinary assistance is essential.

What Should You Do?

The best defense against heatstroke is to monitor your dog and his activities. Do not place him in a situation in which he can become overheated. Limit exercise, such as running, walking, jogging, retrieving, and training to the cooler parts of the day. If your dog is experiencing symptoms of heatstroke, get him to a cool environment immediately. Lower his temperature by submerging his body in cool (not cold) water (keeping his head elevated above water) or applying cool water to his body with a shower or hose. If he will drink on his own, give him water or a rehydrating solution. Do not force water, because he is likely to choke. Place him on a wet towel to keep him cool, and get medical assistance immediately.

Poisoning

"An ounce of prevention…." So goes the saying. That said, accidents do happen, and if you suspect your dog has come in contact with a poisonous substance, treat it as a medical emergency. Do not delay—seek immediate veterinary attention. If you see your dog eating or drinking a poisonous substance, do not wait for symptoms to develop. Call the Poison Control Center or take your dog to the nearest veterinary clinic. Do not induce vomiting unless instructed by a veterinarian.

The best defense against heatstroke is to monitor your dog and his activities; do not place him in a situation where he can become overheated.

Treatment varies depending on the type of poison ingested. Take with you, if possible, the remains of the toxic product, be it a half-eaten plant, a mangled snail bait package, or a half-eaten box of chocolates. If your dog has vomited, scoop it up and take it with you. It can provide the veterinarian with important clues regarding the type of poison your dog ingested.

Vomiting and Diarrhea

It is not unusual for dogs to vomit occasionally, and they can do so with little discomfort. Dogs vomit when they get excited, drink too much water too fast—especially after exercise—gulp their food, go for a ride in the car, or after they've eaten grass. If your dog appears to be healthy, a single vomiting incident should not send you rushing to the vet. It may be nothing more than a simple upset stomach. Keep him away from any food for a few hours. You can allow him small amounts of water, but don't allow him to gulp. Nothing makes a vomiting dog vomit more than a tummy full of water or food. If the problem persists, especially with puppies or old dogs, or if your dog has other symptoms, such as diarrhea, stomach bloating, listlessness, labored breathing, pain, or you see blood in the vomit or abnormal material, contact your veterinarian right away. And don't forget to take a sample of the vomit with you.

Diarrhea can occur if you overfeed your dog, if you change his normal food from one brand to another too quickly, or if there is a change in water while traveling. (It is always prudent to carry your own water or purchase bottled water.) Unclean feeding bowls, stress, and allergies also can cause diarrhea. It also can be a symptom of intestinal parasites or disease.

Normal feces vary in color and consistency depending on the individual dog and his diet. Normal color usually ranges from light brown to dark brown. If the diarrhea is slight, and your dog has no other symptoms, it may be nothing more than minor gastric upset. Withholding food for 24 hours, and then feeding a mixture of cooked white rice and extra lean hamburger browned in a skillet with excess grease removed, may correct the problem. Medications such as bismuth subsalicylate (Pepto-Bismol) or kaolin/pectin (Kaopectate) every 4 hours may also fix the problem. It is always wise to consult your veterinarian before giving any human medications to your dog. Your veterinarian will be able to give you the correct dosage, as well. If you have a puppy or older dog with diarrhea, or if the diarrhea is black or green, or your dog is showing other signs of illness, call your veterinarian right away.

Nonexertion Heatstroke

Your Rottweiler need not run around like a wild banshee in the heat of the day to be susceptible to heatstroke. Nonexertion heatstroke most commonly occurs when a dog is confined in an overheated enclosure, such as an automobile, or when he is confined outdoors during warm weather or high humidity and deprived of water or shade.

Checking for Dehydration

Dogs with diarrhea are susceptible to dehydration, so keep a close eye on your Rottweiler. To check for dehydration, lift the skin at the scruff of his neck between your thumb and index finger, and pull it up an inch or so. Hold it there for a few seconds and let it go. If your dog is not dehydrated, the skin will spring back quickly and flatten out. If he is dehydrated, the skin will stay in a little ridge and take a few seconds to flatten out. If the skin does not flatten out at all and remains looking like a tent, your dog has an extreme medical emergency. Seek veterinary attention right away.

You can also examine your Rottweiler's gums. They should be a healthy pinkish color and moist. If your dog's gums are pale and dry, contact your veterinarian.

Wild Animals

Skunks and porcupines are not generally life threatening, although an encounter with either can be quite traumatic for both

Rottweilers are considered "seniors" anywhere from age six and older.

dog and owner. There is no mistaking the pungent odor of skunk musk. If your Rottweiler has the misfortune of being skunked, bathe him right away. Skunk musk can cause severe eye irritation, so flush his eyes liberally with clear, cool water.

Skunk musk is a persistent and difficult smell to remove—to say the least! The odor also can be transferred to your hands, so wear rubber gloves before touching your pet. Bathing your dog in tomato juice or diluted lemon juice helps eliminate some of the odor, but it won't get rid of it completely. Others have had good luck with an over-the-counter product called Skunk-Off. Some highly recommend bathing a dog with the feminine douche product Massengill, and then bathing him again with a mild baby shampoo.

Overly curious Rottweilers are likely to end up with a face full of porcupine quills, which can be quite painful. Porcupines can have as many as 30,000 quills. They do not "shoot" their quills at dogs, but rather turn their back, raise the quills, and lash out at the dog with their tail. If the porcupine hits the dog with the quills, they become embedded in the dog's skin, usually his face. If your Rottweiler has only a few embedded quills, count yourself lucky! You can try to remove them with a pair of pliers, but more often than not a trip to the veterinarian's is in order. A veterinarian usually anesthetizes your precious pooch to remove the quills and minimize discomfort. Dogs don't seem to learn their lesson, and they are quite eager to repeat their little escapade again and again.

THE SENIOR ROTTWEILER

Rottweilers are considered "seniors" anywhere from age 6 years and older. You are the best judge of when to make this call for your dog. You will notice when he begins to slow down, is not interested in long walks around the neighborhood, sleeps more, and seems to be getting gray around the muzzle. Your veterinarian may also notice signs that indicate it is time to consider these your dog's golden years.

Many owners say that this time of their dog's life is the most enjoyable, because their dogs have a routine, they know the family, and they know what to expect. Older dogs tend to be less active, which means you do not need to keep up with them, and they are more interested than ever in curling up next to you on the couch.

With good care your Rottweiler can be a fun companion for years to come.

Old age has its requirements, though, just as puppyhood did. Assess your dog's overall health and determine what you need to do to maintain it as its peak, which could include:

- Changing his diet to one specially formulated for seniors.
- Supplementing his food with certain vitamins, minerals, or herbs for improved skin condition or healthier joints.
- Keeping him warm and providing him a draft-free area to sleep will help to keep stiff joints and sore muscles to a minimum.

Mind how you interact with your senior citizen. His eyesight or hearing may be failing before it is readily apparent, so be sure he hears and sees you when you ask him to do things. His bladder control may weaken, leading to accidents in the house. These are probably as upsetting to him as to you; have patience—remember, your friend won't live forever. Treasure him while you can!

RESOURCES

BREED CLUBS

Allgemeiner Deutscher Rottweiler Klub (ARDK)
Nordrhein-Westfalen
32429 Minden
Südring 18
Germany
E-mail: info@adrk.de
www.adrk.de

American Kennel Club (AKC)
5580 Centerview Drive
Raleigh, NC 27606
Telephone: (919) 233-9767
Fax: (919) 233-3627
E-mail: info@akc.org
www.akc.org

American Rottweiler Club (ARC)
Secretary: Diane Garnett
E-mail: garnets@att.net
www.amrottclub.org

American Rottweiler Verein (ARV)
Membership Director: Jenny Salquist
E-mail: jenecks20@aol.com
www.arv.org

Canadian Kennel Club (CKC)
89 Skyway Avenue, Suite 100
Etobicoke, Ontario M9W 6R4
Telephone: (416) 675-5511
Fax: (416) 675-6506
E-mail: information@ckc.ca
www.ckc.ca

Federation Cynologique Internationale (FCI)
Secretariat General de la FCI
Place Albert 1er, 13
B – 6530 Thuin
Belqique
www.fci.be

The Kennel Club
1 Clarges Street
London
W1J 8AB
Telephone: 0870 606 6750
Fax: 0207 518 1058
www.the-kennel-club.org.uk

United Kennel Club (UKC)
100 E. Kilgore Road
Kalamazoo, MI 49002-5584
Telephone: (269) 343-9020
Fax: (269) 343-7037
E-mail: pbickell@ukcdogs.com
www.ukcdogs.com

United States Rottweiler Club (USRC)
Secretary: Laurie Stupak
E-mail: secretary@usrconline.org
www.usrconline.org

RESCUE ORGANIZATIONS AND ANIMAL WELFARE GROUPS

American Humane Association (AHA)
63 Inverness Drive East
Englewood, CO 80112
Telephone: (303) 792-9900
Fax: 792-5333
www.americanhumane.org

American Society for the Prevention of Cruelty to Animals (ASPCA)
424 E. 92nd Street
New York, NY 10128-6804
Telephone: (212) 876-7700
www.aspca.org

Royal Society for the Prevention of Cruelty to Animals (RSPCA)
Telephone: 0870 3335 999
Fax: 0870 7530 284
www.rspca.org.uk

The Humane Society of the United States (HSUS)
2100 L Street, NW
Washington DC 20037
Telephone: (202) 452-1100
www.hsus.org

SPORTS

Canine Freestyle Federation, Inc.
Secretary: Brandy Clymire
E-Mail: secretary@canine-freestyle.org
www.canine-freestyle.org

International Agility Link (IAL)
Global Administrator: Steve Drinkwater
E-mail: yunde@powerup.au
www.agilityclick.com/~ial
International Weight Pull Association
E-mail: info@iwpa.net
www.iwpa.net

North American Dog Agility Council
11522 South Hwy 3
Cataldo, ID 83810
www.nadac.com

North American Flyball Association (NAFA)
1400 West Devon Avenue #512
Chicago, IL 60660
Telephone: (800) 318-6312
Fax: (800) 318-6318
www.flyball.org

United Schutzhund Clubs of America (USA)
3810 Paule Ave.
St. Louis, MO 63125-1718
Telephone: (314) 638-9686
Fax: (314) 638-0609
www.germanshepherddog.com

United States Dog Agility Association
P.O. Box 850955
Richardson, TX 75085-0955
Telephone: (972) 487-2200
www.usdaa.com

World Canine Freestyle Organization
P.O. Box 350122
Brooklyn, NY 11235-2525
Telephone: (718) 332-8336
www.worldcaninefreestyle.org

VETERINARY AND HEALTH RESOURCES

Academy of Veterinary Homeopathy (AVH)
P.O. Box 9280
Wilmington, DE 19809
Telephone: (866) 652-1590
Fax: (866) 652-1590
E-mail: office@TheAVH.org
www.theavh.org

American Academy of Veterinary Acupuncture (AAVA)
100 Roscommon Drive, Suite 320
Middletown, CT 06457
Telephone: (860) 635-6300
Fax: (860) 635-6400
E-mail: office@aava.org
www.aava.org

American Animal Hospital Association (AAHA)
P.O. Box 150899
Denver, CO 80215-0899
Telephone: (303) 986-2800
Fax: (303) 986-1700
E-mail: info@aahanet.org
www.aahanet.org/index.cfm

American College of Veterinary Internal Medicine (ACVIM)
1997 Wadsworth Blvd., Suite A
Lakewood, CO 80214-5293
Telephone: (800) 245-9081
Fax: (303) 231-0880
Email: ACVIM@ACVIM.org
www.acvim.org

American College of Veterinary Ophthalmologists (ACVO)
P.O. Box 1311
Meridian, Idaho 83860
Telephone: (208) 466-7624
Fax: (208) 466-7693
E-mail: office@acvo.com
www.acvo.com

American Heartworm Society
PO Box 667
Batavia, IL 60510
E-mail: heartwormsociety@earthlink.net
www.heartwormsociety.org

American Holistic Veterinary Medical Association (AHVMA)
2218 Old Emmorton Road
Bel Air, MD 21015
Telephone: (410) 569-0795
Fax: (410) 569-2346
E-mail: office@ahvma.org
www.ahvma.org

American Veterinary Medical Association (AVMA)
1931 North Meacham Road – Suite 100
Schaumburg, IL 60173
Telephone: (847) 925-8070
Fax: (847) 925-1329
E-mail: avmainfo@avma.org
www.avma.org

ASPCA Animal Poison Control Center
1717 South Philo Road, Suite 36
Urbana, IL 61802
Telephone: (888) 426-4435
www.aspca.org

British Veterinary Association (BVA)
7 Mansfield Street
London
W1G 9NQ
Telephone: 020 7636 6541
Fax: 020 7436 2970
E-mail: bvahq@bva.co.uk
www.bva.co.uk

Rottweiler Health Foundation
5215 Holston Hills Road
Knoxville, TN 37914
E-mail: info@rottweilerhealth.org
www.rottweilerhealth.org

ACKNOWLEDGEMENTS

A special thanks to my husband, Paul, whose love and encouragement have been the constant in my life, enabling me to the opportunity to write and train dogs every day. Special thanks to Pam Grant, president, American Rottweiler Club; C.A. Sharp for her research and for unselfishly sharing her expertise; Colin Sealy at the Kennel Club (UK) for his research; and all of the interesting and remarkable ARC members and owners I have had the good fortune to speak with along the way. There have been so many that to mention them all would fill an entire book. To Bobbie Anderson and Sylvia Bishop for their training, insight and words of wisdom, and to Heather Russell-Revesz at TFH Publications, Inc., for her guidance.

ABOUT THE AUTHOR

Tracy Libby is an award-winning freelance writer and author of *Building Blocks for Performance* (Alpine 2002). Her articles have appeared in numerous publications, including the *AKC Gazette, Puppies USA, You and Your Dog,* and *Dog Fancy's Popular Dogs* series. She is a member of the Dog Writers Association of America and a recipient of the Ellsworth S. Howell award for distinguished dog writing. She lives in Oregon, and has been involved in the sport of dogs for 20 years, exhibiting in conformation and obedience.

PHOTO CREDITS

Photo on page 52 courtesy of Paulette Braun
Photo on page 93 courtesy of LucyAnn Dyck (Shutterstock)
Photo on page 48 courtesy of Eric Isseleé (Shutterstock)
Photo on page 47 courtesy of Joy Miller (Shutterstock)
Photo on page 24 courtesy of Gordana Sermek (Shutterstock)
Photo on page 136 courtesy of George Shagawat
Photo on page 38 courtesy of Brenda Arlene Smith (Shutterstock)
Photos on pages 99, 139 courtesy of Julie Snyder
Photos on pages 36, 37, 56, 90, 92, 160 courtesy of Lara Stern
All other photos courtesy of Isabelle Francais and TFH archives

A